GENDERED REPUTATIONS AND ARISTOCRATIC PARTNERSHIP

GENDER AND POWER IN THE PREMODERN WORLD

Further Information and Publications

www.arc-humanities.org/series/book-series/

GENDERED REPUTATIONS AND ARISTOCRATIC PARTNERSHIP

RE-PRESENTING THE BRETON CIVIL WAR FROM THE FOURTEENTH TO SIXTEENTH CENTURIES

by

ERIKA GRAHAM-GOERING

ARC HUMANITIES PRESS

British Library Cataloguing in Publication Data
A catalogue record for this book is available from the British Library.

ISBN (Hardback): 9781641894081
ISBN (Paperback): 9781802703610
e-ISBN (PDF): 9781802702361
e-ISBN (ePUB): 9781802703603

www.arc-humanities.org

Printed and bound in the UK (by CPIGroup [UK] Ltd), USA (by Bookmasters), and elsewhere using print-on-demand technology.

Publisher (manufacturer) details: Arc Humanities Press, 14 Clifton Moor Business Village, James Nicolson Link, York YO30 4XG, United Kingdom.

EU Authorized Representative details (for GPSR purposes): Amsterdam University Press, Nieuwe Prinsengracht 89, 1018 VR Amsterdam, The Netherlands. www.aup.nl

To Roan Emeric

CONTENTS

PREFACE

I AM GREATLY obliged to my MA and PhD supervisor at York, Craig Taylor, who got me started down this path by listening to my disjointed first impressions of Charles's canonization process, then pointing out, "It sounds like you're interested in reputation." This insight, and the guidance he generously gave me as I went on to figure out what that meant, has been invaluable.

My understanding of what I was trying to do in this book has also been profoundly shaped by the many students I've been lucky to teach at the universities of York, Ghent, Durham, and Oslo. Thank you for all our conversations and for sharing the learning journey.

As this project developed across many hurdles of the modern "early career researcher" life (let alone the coronavirus pandemic), I deeply appreciate everyone who made the path less precarious and the work less stressful. Foremost among these is Frederik Buylaert, who fostered my postdoctoral career at Ghent University (where I first hatched the cunning plan of writing two books instead of one), and with whom I feel privileged to have worked. Ellie Woodacre (who also gave valuable comments on the completed draft) and Danna Messer were instrumental in bringing what I thought would be a quick little study to Arc Humanities Press, where Tania Colwell has shepherded me through the later stages of publication. I sincerely appreciate all their support and patience.

For their technical expertise, I would like to thank Laura Macy for the copy-editing, Martine Maguire-Weltecke for the typesetting, and Sally Osborn for the index. Open Access to this book was made possible thanks to the FWO (Research Foundation – Flanders), under grant 12ZX221N. The preliminary stages of this research were additionally funded by the Overseas Student Scholarship and Overseas Research Scholarship schemes of the University of York.

Kristin Bourassa, Godfried Croenen, Pierre Courroux, Steffen Hope, Chloë R. McKenzie, Hartley Miller, Hans Jacob Orning, Graeme Small, Tess Wingard, and Claudia Wittig nobly tackled my niche questions, shared their work, and offered me their thoughtful feedback and advice throughout the writing process. I consider myself incredibly fortunate to be able to call such kind and clever scholars my friends and colleagues, along with many others not named here.

Last but not least, I remain so, so grateful for the love and encouragement of my family. Look, the book is finally done! My thanks go especially to my husband Nelson Goering, who is the best partner I could ever wish to have.

ABBREVIATIONS OF PRIMARY SOURCES

The following short forms are used to refer to the core primary sources analyzed in this book. References to the editorial introduction or critical apparatus use standard citations instead of abbreviations.

Abridged — Froissart, Jean. *Œuvres de Froissart: Chroniques*. Edited by J.-B.-M.-C. Kervyn de Lettenhove. Devaux, 1867–1877. Vol. 17 (1872).

Amiens — Froissart, Jean. *Chroniques: Livre I, le manuscrit d'Amiens*. Edited by George T. Diller. 5 vols. Droz, 1991–1998.

Chanson — Cuvelier. *La chanson de Bertrand du Guesclin de Cuvelier*. Edited by Jean-Claude Faucon. Vol. 1. Éditions universitaires du Sud, 1990.

D — [Depositions from] Héry, Laurent, Jean-Paul Le Guillou, Yves Le Guillou, Armelle Le Huërou, and André Vauchez, eds. *Le procès de canonisation de Charles de Blois, duc de Bretagne (1319–1364)*. Vol. 1, *Le procès d'Angers (1371)*. Presses universitaires de Rennes, 2023.

FrB — Froissart, Jean. *Chroniques de J. Froissart*. Edited by Siméon Luce. 11 vols. Renouard, 1869–1899.

GCB — Bouchart, Alain. *Les grandes croniques de Bretaigne*. Edited by Marie-Louise Auger, Gustave Jeanneau, and Bernard Guenée. 2 vols. Centre national de la recherche scientifique, 1998.

LBC — Le Baud, Pierre. *Compillation des cronicques et ystoires des Bretons*. Edited by Karine Abélard. Presses universitaires de Rennes, 2018.

LBG — Le Baud, Pierre. "La '*Genealogie des roys, ducs et princes de Bretaigne*' de Pierre Le Baud (1486)," edited by Jean Kerhervé. In *Bretagne et pays celtiques: Langues, histoire, civilisation. Mélanges offerts à la mémoire de Léon Fleuriot*, edited by Gwennolé Le Menn and Jean-Yves Le Moing, 519–60. Presses universitaires de Rennes, 1992.

LBH — Le Baud, Pierre. *Histoire de Bretagne, avec les chroniques des maisons de Vitré et de Laval*. Edited by C. d'Hosier. Alliot, 1638.

PGA — Ménard, Claude, ed. *Histoire de messire Bertrand du Guesclin, connestable de France*. Cramoisy, 1618.

PGB — Buchon, J.-A.-C., ed. "Chronique anonyme de sire Bertrand du Guesclin." In *Choix de chroniques et mémoires sur l'histoire de France*, 4:1–95. Desrez, 1839.

Rome — Froissart, Jean. *Chroniques: Dernière rédaction du premier livre, édition du manuscrit de Rome Reg. lat. 869*. Edited by George T. Diller. Droz, 1972.

INTRODUCTION

THIS BOOK EXPLORES how aristocratic leadership was understood in response to the political conflicts of the late Middle Ages. It focuses on how elite audiences engaged with different ideas about men's and women's joint authority as a way to make sense of these clashes. Tracing the development of this discourse in a case study across the fourteenth to sixteenth centuries, I argue that the tensions defining political society encouraged a perpetual reassessment of the dynamics of legitimate power, which became comparative rather than categorical.

The protagonists, so to speak, of this analysis are Charles de Blois (ca. 1321–1364) and Jeanne de Penthièvre (ca. 1326–1384), duke and duchess of Brittany in what is now northwestern France. Jeanne was the niece of the previous duke, Jean III, while her husband Charles was the nephew of the king of France, Philippe VI. Jeanne was expected to succeed her childless uncle to the Breton title in 1341, but her half-uncle Jean de Montfort challenged her claim. Despite winning the legal confirmation of her rights from the king's *parlement* at Paris, the support of King Edward III of England for her rival led to war. Jeanne and Charles controlled much of the duchy for over two decades, but their authority faced repeated disruptions, including several major military defeats, Charles's capture and nine-year imprisonment in England, and the surrender of two sons and one daughter as hostages for his ransom. The conflict abated only after Charles died at the battle of Auray in 1364 and Jeanne signed a treaty recognizing Jean de Montfort's son as Duke Jean IV in 1365. Nevertheless, she remained titular duchess and pursued an active political career for the rest of her life.

I am not concerned here, however, with the events or even the rhetoric of Jeanne and Charles's actual exercise of power, which I have analyzed primarily from Jeanne's perspective elsewhere.[1] Instead, I am interested in what other people had to say about their authority after the fact. From the 1370s to the 1510s (and beyond), many commentators reflected on, repurposed, and repackaged the events of the Breton civil war and its controversial duke and duchess to meet the political needs of the moment. Because

1 Graham-Goering, *Princely Power*.

these accounts used codified social categories to communicate efficiently, they reveal the range of values associated with different models of power, from knights and princesses to saints, parents, and lords. However, there was also friction between—and indeed within—these ideals. How and why were such tensions magnified or resolved by talking about two people together instead of just one?

Concepts

The conceptual framework supporting this study can be broken down along the lines suggested by its title. I focus on the primary historiographical questions underpinning each component and how the case of Jeanne and Charles can contribute towards addressing them, rather than attempting any exhaustive citation of these diverse and rapidly developing fields.

Aristocratic Partnership

An aristocratic partnership implies, in essence, a power-sharing relationship, but within the broad scope of the political, social, and cultural authority this elite could wield, certain dynamics are of particular interest. I refer throughout this book to Jeanne and Charles's "leadership" as a neutral umbrella term that takes in both the active capacity for decision-making and command, and the ability to attract loyalty as the legitimate authority. However, I also draw attention to more specific manifestations of hierarchy that marked the late Middle Ages. Lordship, first, was seen as the common denominator of all domination, from God above, through kings and barons, down to husbands in their households; it was, as Rees Davies puts it, "part of the natural order of the universe."[2] There is a tendency, though, for lordship to get buried within the rubric of kingship at a higher level and that of nobility at the lower, rather than understood as a context for power-sharing in its own right. Because we so often take lordship for granted, much of the methodology and theory of its study remains to be adequately developed, but meanwhile, looking at reputation can help pinpoint some important ways contemporaries engaged with the concept and the challenges it posed as an ideal even at the time. I will also speak of "rulership" to highlight the preeminent position of lords at the level of a principality such as Brittany, especially given the huge influence of royal studies on political history, but such princes were also part of a continuum. A second thematic focus is the

---

2 Davies, *Lords and Lordship*, 16.

concept of knighthood, numerically declining in this period but still essential to aristocratic identities.[3] Idealized knighthood had two facets of interest here.[4] On one hand, knights exemplified martial skill, and on the other they offered faithful service to their superiors. Its particular functions gave knighthood a distinct relationship to power from lordship, but both frameworks fed into shaping the dynamics of partnership.

Historians are fortunately moving beyond viewing political power in the Middle Ages as primarily autocratic to emphasize its collaborative aspects. This shift has been particularly noticeable in how we study monarchy. Ernst Kantorowicz famously advanced the idea that the Crown had a "corporational character," involving not only the king but also the great magnates who helped him govern.[5] This relatively abstract framing has become more concrete as historians explore the forms of royal power-sharing taken in various contexts.[6] To give only a few examples particularly relevant to medieval Europe, the kingship itself could be parcelled out, with different members of the ruling family each having at least a potential claim to authority.[7] While the field of candidates might narrow over time, such shifts should not be taken as a move away from corporate monarchy itself, but rather towards other solutions for sharing power. Kings might rule alongside their designated son and successor during their own lifetimes in a form of associative kingship.[8] The system of apanages in Capetian France, where younger sons received large territories within the kingdom to govern rather than dividing the realm and title, nevertheless ensured that what Graeme Small calls the "royal familial community" would be the major driver of French politics throughout the fourteenth and fifteenth centuries.[9] And whereas queens were traditionally seen as peripheral accessories to the king, especially in the high and later medieval periods, we now recognize them as an integral part of a ruling partnership.[10] Theresa Earenfight lays out the consequences of

3 Contamine, "Points de vue"; Taylor, *Chivalry and the Ideals of Knighthood.*

4 Cf. Karras, *From Boys to Men*, 24–25.

5 Kantorowicz, *King's Two Bodies*, 381.

6 Woodacre, "Understanding the Mechanisms of Monarchy," 12.

7 Spangler, "Family Affair," 469–71; Naderer, "Love and Fear," 69–76.

8 Whaley, "From *a* Salic Law to *the* Salic Law"; Martin, "Anticipatory Association of the Heir."

9 Wood, *French Apanages*; Small, *Late Medieval France.*

10 See Woodacre, *Queens Regnant*; and Beem and Taylor, *Man Behind the Queen*, for just two examples from the plethora of recent studies.

this interpretation particularly clearly when she characterizes rulership as "a malleable, permeable and multivocal political institution that can be envisioned, metaphorically speaking, as a flexible sack."[11] Monarchy, in apparent contradiction to its name, was not the rule of one: the only question was how wide it might stretch, and this question was never permanently settled.

The implications for power dynamics below the level of monarchy have been somewhat slower in coming, though the field is clearly headed in this direction. There is increasing evidence, for instance, that even married women could exercise direct power within the aristocracy and wider elites.[12] More broadly, since we know that medieval socio-political power fundamentally relied on networks of all kinds, it is surprising that we still often assume that methods for distributing power such as multiple lordship and co-lordship were deviations from normal or desirable practice.[13] Nevertheless, such patterns of power-sharing as part of general seigneurial practices are starting to gain more serious attention.[14] It is also telling that most studies across these areas focus on the period 1000–1300 (or even earlier), leaving the later Middle Ages to be dominated by the "rise of the state." That narrative has usually stressed the centralization of power, even if state formation has increasingly been reinterpreted as more cooperative than competitive. Just recently, though, the contributions of decentralized and delegated authority to this process have started to come to light.[15] So there is ample room to expand our appreciation of aristocratic collaboration as part not just of how things worked, but how people expected them to work.

Studying the partnership of the duke and duchess of Brittany builds on this discourse in several ways. First, this case study helps translate the frameworks of corporate monarchy into the sphere of the aristocracy at large. Aristocrats, even magnates, faced different pressures from their royal counterparts, since they were unburdened by the extensive ideological baggage of sacral monarchy and occupied a secondary position within the realm's political hierarchy. This distinctive social context affected the manifestation and interpretation of joint leadership. Still, the princes' preemi-

11 Earenfight, "Without the Persona," 10.

12 Livingstone, "Recalculating the Equation"; Tanner, "Women's Legal Capacity"; Tanner, *Medieval Elite Women*; Graham-Goering, *Princely Power*.

13 Althoff, *Family, Friends and Followers*; White, *Re-Thinking Kinship*; Esmark et al., *Nordic Elites*.

14 "Coseigneurie"; Débax, *Seigneurie collective*; Boston, *Lordship and Locality*.

15 Graham-Goering et al., *Lordship and the Decentralized State*.

nent political position on the regional level heightened the common conceptual tools of aristocratic power, making it easier to see how these responded to collaborative dynamics. Second, the timing of the Breton war of succession and its narrative afterlife is useful for bridging the routine boundaries of periodization. Examining how the same actors and events were adapted to new contexts over some 150 years shows both continuity and evolution in assessing shared power. Finally, while this research focuses on Jeanne and Charles as a married couple, this core partnership was closely tied into other relationships, groups, and networks, all of which contributed to defining the meaning and legitimacy of their joint rule. This case can therefore help us connect the different forms of collaboration now being studied as integral to premodern political culture.

Gendered Reputations

Reputation was at this time deeply embedded in many facets of life. Often discussed under the Latin name of *fama* (whence English "fame"), it meant in broad terms what was widely known about someone, but such public information had serious consequences.[16] While the personal and professional ramifications of having a good or bad name in most social contexts are perhaps readily grasped, there was a particular truth value to "that which is commonly said, held, and told" that gained evidentiary weight in all sorts of legal proceedings during this period.[17] Reputation was also a tool for community social monitoring and enforcing behavioural norms, ostensibly in aid of the common good.[18] Correspondingly, public opinion had real political force from both above and below, a factor that has fed into an increasingly expansive view of later medieval political society.[19] For the nobility in particular, reputation was vital to justifying both individual honour and collective domination, and I will focus here primarily on how this concern offers a new approach to the issues surrounding the aristocratic marital partnership.

---

16 Arbelet and Devlaeminck, "Fama"; Soria and Billoré, *Rumeur au Moyen Âge*; Fenster and Smail, *Fama*; Gauvard, "Renommée"; cf. Walker and Kerr, *"Fama" and her Sisters.*

17 Théry-Astruc, "*Fama*" (also in English translation); Gauvard, "*Fama* explicite et *fama* implicite."

18 Coleman, "Scholastic Treatments," 24–25.

19 Guenée, *Opinion publique*; Dumolyn et al., *Voices of the People*; Slater, "Rumour and Reputation Management"; Théry-Astruc, "*Fama*"; Genet, "Political Society"; Watts, "Pressure of the Public."

Gender underpins this discussion on two levels. While the full complexity of medieval gender lies beyond my present scope, the analysis of elite reputation is impacted by questions of (1) what men and women were said to have done, and/or (2) how their actions were characterized as masculine or feminine (or both or neither).[20] I examine both sides of this coin in the narratives surrounding Jeanne and Charles's partnership. Such an emphasis is not to say that gender was uniquely significant in determining reputation, but its importance as "*a* primary way of signifying relationships of power" raises problems of particular relevance to the interpretation of joint leadership.[21] Christopher Fletcher has, moreover, pointed out the need "to bring gender history and political history together, taking both politics and gender equally seriously," a task which has so far proceeded unevenly.[22]

I hope to make two main contributions by examining shared power from the perspective of gendered reputations. First, reputation is an especially sensitive instrument for gauging the cultural and political importance contemporaries attached to power-sharing between men and women. In Rhiannon Snaith's formulation, "expectation lay at the root of reputation; the ability to meet expectation resulted in praise and positive renown, while failure to live up to the same ideal was punished by criticism."[23] Focusing on reputation clarifies how legitimate authority was constructed and evaluated, a process that, Jean-Philippe Genet argues, "is less self-evident for the medieval period than we might think."[24] At the same time, aristocratic ideals (just like gendered ones) were a moving target rather than a static metric, so that pinning them down was a constant yet inconclusive challenge. Medieval aristocrats tried to carefully control their *fama* using a range of methods to influence public discourse, sometimes successfully, sometimes less so. As Craig Taylor shows, efforts to convey these principles necessarily also had a hand in shaping the ongoing debate.[25] Studying reputation therefore provides an important complement to the practical dynamics of co-rule,

20 I focus here on the most salient gender categories in my source material; for a recent survey and discussion of non-binary medieval history, see Wingard, "Trans Middle Ages."

21 Quote from Scott, *Gender and the Politics of History*, 44 (my italics). Cf. LoPrete, "Women, Gender and Lordship," 1925; Waag, "Rulership, Authority, and Power," 103.

22 Fletcher, "Introduction."

23 Snaith, "Politics of Noble Reputation," 30.

24 Genet, "Pouvoir symbolique," 10.

25 Taylor, *Virtuous Knight*, 5.

because it speaks to how and why it was normalized or contested in different political contexts.

Second, and conversely, spousal power-sharing can help us synthesize several strands within the study of political reputations. Historians now recognize that monarchy necessarily contained both masculine and feminine elements. These could be encapsulated within the single figure of the monarch, as in Cynthia Herrup's argument that early modern rulers could "inhabit an artificial body that was gendered neither exclusively male nor female, but both," but were more usually parcelled out between the king and queen who jointly constructed royal power.[26] Yet most studies of royal reputations foreground either the king or queen rather than both together, a problem that Henric Bagerius and Christine Ekholst have also highlighted.[27] Likewise among the wider aristocracy, scholarship on reputation has usually dealt more with individuals or family lineages than with partnerships, and so missed a key link in the chain. (I strongly suspect that part of this individual focus comes from the close relationship between the projects of reputation and biography.) As a result, while the reputations of both men and women as rulers were shaped by similar normative categories, including appropriate sexual behaviour, use of power, honourable conduct, and so on, these parallels and their reciprocal influence across genders have not been fully examined.

Moreover, the focus on individual reputations has only reinforced tendencies to study the ideals of women's and men's authority separately. The two fields, after all, have had markedly different trajectories. Medieval masculinities (quickly pluralized in a way that "femininities" rarely are) have received serious attention only from the 1990s, as a response to the growth of women's studies in the preceding decades, and there are no signs of achieving balanced attention to men within medieval gender scholarship any time soon.[28] Starting at the top of the political hierarchy, the boom in queenship studies since the 1960s and especially the 1980s has only much more recently been matched by interest in kingship as a specifically gendered phenomenon, as Katherine Lewis astutely explains.[29] To some extent,

26 Herrup, "King's Two Genders," 496.

27 Bagerius and Ekholst, "Unruly Queen," 103.

28 Lees, *Medieval Masculinities*; Hadley, *Masculinity*; Murray, *Conflicted Identities*. As an extremely crude metric, works dealing with women/femininity versus men/masculinity available on the International Medieval Bibliography on August 14, 2024 show a ratio of about 5:1, a trend that has held remarkably steady since the '90s.

29 Lewis, *Kingship and Masculinity*, 3–5; cf. Fletcher, *Richard II*.

this separate treatment is justified by the historical reality. Although we know there is clear overlap between the actual practices of men and women's lordship, the conceptual frameworks of gender were embedded within hierarchies of power.[30] Historians have shown how manliness was in many ways constructed through competition and comparison not with women, but with other men in elite homosocial contexts.[31] Meanwhile, the spotlight put on ruling women has been instrumental in making their roles visible to us despite their frequent relegation to a secondary status.[32] Although calls for greater attention to the co-production of gender are not new, nor have they gone wholly unanswered, the impact on political history remains limited.[33]

Nevertheless, a blended approach to reputation is needed to fully appreciate the political world of the aristocracy as a whole. Claudia Wittig's work on the transmission of idealized conduct in high medieval courts, for example, shows the benefits of integrating analysis of the expectations set upon young noblemen and -women to understand how "communities of values" came to be.[34] Because spousal power-sharing necessarily set male and female actors, and masculine and feminine performances of power, side-by-side, it is an especially effective context to examine how the gendering of each reputation influenced the other. Necessarily, my discussion of certain aspects of Jeanne's and Charles's reputations will prioritize only one person, to better unpick how they were affected by complicated ideals of gender and power. But I consistently return to what I call *relational* reputations, by which I mean both the mutual impact of two individual reputations on one another, and how the relationship between two individuals was a deliberate strategy of reputation-building. Through such comparison, reputation itself becomes, rather than just "a singular property that shapes the place of the individual in...a society of honour," a product of power-sharing.[35]

---

30 LoPrete, "Women, Gender and Lordship"; Evergates, *Aristocracy in the County of Champagne*.

31 Karras, *From Boys to Men*, esp. 10–11; Lewis, *Kingship and Masculinity*, 7; McVitty, "False Knights"; Storey, "Questioning Terminologies."

32 See Woodacre, *Queens and Queenship*, for an accessible synopsis of the main findings of this scholarship to date.

33 Rasmussen, *Rivalrous Masculinities*; Lewis, *Kingship and Masculinity*, 10, 59.

34 Wittig, *Learning to Be Noble*.

35 Gauvard, "*Fama* explicite et *fama* implicite," 39.

Civil War

I analyze shared power in the context of conflict, which has several implications for my scope and conclusions. As a war of succession, the case study of Brittany fits into our usual ideas about what a civil war is: a conflict internal to a given polity and fought ultimately over control of that polity. This clear-cut categorization can be challenged, however, on both specific and general grounds. If Bretons fought against Bretons in support of rival would-be dukes, the involvement of the kings of France and of England made Brittany a proxy for the sprawling dispute retroactively dubbed the Hundred Years' War. The combatants in the duchy were heterogeneous in their origins and affiliations, including not only English and French lords but Genoese mercenaries and Spanish adventurers. Meanwhile, Charles and Jeanne themselves were also viscount and viscountess of Limoges to the south, equally contested by the Montforts yet with few direct links to Brittany.[36] And although the conventional dates for the war are 1341–1365, and these do identify a meaningful chapter at least concerning the legal basis for conflict, the Penthièvre–Montfort rivalry had no definitive settlement until the late fifteenth century (as we will see), so speaking of *the* war of succession is also something of an artifice.

More broadly, historians, political scientists, and anthropologists have questioned the category of "civil war" itself. I draw here especially on the recent synthesis and new insights developed in the project *The Nordic "Civil Wars" in the High Middle Ages in a Comparative Perspective*.[37] This research takes on board not only critiques of defining civil war as somehow exceptional compared to other wars, but also the pushback against seeing violence as a sign of breakdown in itself. These scholars argue that "war, civil war, rebellion, succession dispute, etc. should not automatically be seen as challenging or indeed undermining the socio-political order, but rather be conceived of as the very vehicles through which the polycentric order of medieval polities and politics played out."[38] Taking endemic violence as politically normative rather than disruptive does not mean that it was never seen as problematic. To the contrary, the potential for violence to regulate

36 Graham-Goering, "Une principauté décentrée?"; Coativy and Massoni, "Vicomté de Limoges."

37 Sigurðsson and Orning, introduction to *Medieval and Modern Civil Wars*, ix–xiv; Comaroff, "Reflections."

38 Orning et al., *New Perspectives*, 344; cf. Lantschner, *Logic of Political Conflict*; Challet, "Violence as a Political Language."

the social order meant that its legitimacy was necessarily open to scrutiny and debate. What this premise does mean is that war and peace were not a strict dichotomy. Instead, medieval (and indeed, many other) societies existed in what may be called "constant crisis."[39] This concept encapsulates how tension could escalate into outright conflict or could abate, but was never fully resolved; or, to put it another way, war was the intensification of politics as usual in such highly networked societies.

I will continue to refer to the Breton war of succession as a civil war for three reasons. First, it remains a convenient shorthand for the period of acute tensions in the mid-fourteenth century that was marked by military campaigning and disputed political authority. Second, this conflict became increasingly distinct in the historiography between then and now, a process kick-started by the sources studied here. How and why different people conceptualized *a* civil war, or pushed back against that framing, is essential in assessing its impact upon narratives of leadership. Third, the narrower definition of civil war as a fight between rivals over political legitimacy explains the value of reputation as a vehicle for spelling out previously implicit norms. Nevertheless, this designation is not meant to put up barriers with what came before or after. Rather, I adopt the framework of constant crisis to draw attention to how conflict called for an ongoing re-evaluation of legitimacy, as well as how the contested succession continued its repercussions over an extended timeframe. By treating crisis as routine rather than exceptional, the Breton case becomes part and parcel of the wider political trends of this period.

The dynamics of ruling partnerships examined through the lens of reputation offer in return a further perspective on this critical framework. The appeal to multiple models of gendered leadership to explain or appraise a conflict shows how even constant crisis was unevenly distributed according to a range of structural criteria that were themselves contested. Likewise, the power couple as a specific node within the wider social connections that drove political interactions deepens our concept of polycentricity and the various horizontal and vertical relationships that structured even later medieval polities. Shared power, far from being a crisis itself, helped perpetuate authority across periods of heightened tension and construct (or deconstruct) its subsequent significance.

Finally, the framework of civil war reflects back on how I understand the aristocratic leadership with which I began. The capacity for violence has

---

39 Orning and Vigh, "Constant Crisis"; Orning, *Constant Crisis*.

played a core role in analyses of medieval politics from the emergence of lordship to that of states.[40] From a gendered perspective, however, noblemen and women had different positions towards violence as both a physical and social possibility. Warfare, as a quintessentially masculine activity, offers an important testing ground for how noblewomen's reputations might be gendered. Conversely, taking men as the baseline has long encouraged a relatively narrow vision of elite medieval violence and military leadership based largely on feats of arms. But women's involvement in the warrior aristocracy shows she needed not *be* a knight to command them. Accordingly, recognizing the ways women contributed to the pursuit of warfare, from generalship to logistics to planning to diplomacy, has led historians to a broader understanding of military matters beyond the battlefield, an insight equally relevant to knights themselves.[41]

Nevertheless, women's status within the knightly martial ethos is far from fully clarified, a pressing need given that as many as one in five lordships were held by women, depending on the time and place.[42] While such entitlement did not automatically translate to active governance (any more than it did for men), neither did women have to inherit power directly to become intimately involved in that world.[43] Christine de Pizan in the early fifteenth century recommended that married noblewomen familiarize themselves not only with every practical aspect of military command, but the interpersonal side too. A baroness should test her soldiers' bravery and determination before fully trusting them, avoid incurring their hatred by pressing them too hard, and encourage their loyalty and prowess with her noble words.[44] Insofar as warfare had come to be *the* field defining aristocratic status (a context perhaps only intensified by competition with the up-and-coming "nobility of the robe" at this time[45]), the reputations of women as well as men necessarily developed in relation to violence. However, this martial identity was embedded within wider structures such as family and inheritance, which could compel obedience and even legitimize violence

40 Bisson et al., "Debate: The 'Feudal Revolution'"; Firnhaber-Baker, *Violence and the State.*

41 Sjursen, "Peaceweavers' Sisters"; Harwood, *Medieval Women and War*; Isaac, "Women in Command."

42 Graham-Goering, "Empowering Lordship," 395–96.

43 Sjursen, "War of the Two Jeannes."

44 Pizan, *Livre des trois vertus*, 149–52.

45 Autrand, "Image de la noblesse."

without being overtly violent in themselves. To capture both the multifaceted nature of warfare and its intersection with these other components of constant crisis, I will analyze reputations for leadership across a range of contexts, not strictly in relation to the fighting itself. This broad-brush approach will help clarify the political legitimization of men and women alike within the warrior aristocracy.

Sources and Approach

Taking reputation as an analytical scope means leaning into, rather than working around, the agendas of the available sources. Reputation could not be built in a vacuum: it required corroboration, in two senses. On one hand, elites relied extensively on material, visual, and textual resources to craft their image.[46] On the other, these claims had to reach, and persuade, an audience, who might have ideas of their own. The narratives that have come down to us, the ones recorded in a durable form, can have a disproportionate impact on modern historiography compared to their success at the time.[47] However, while Thelma Fenster and Daniel Lord Smail contrast unstable, spoken *fama* with the "fixed, unchanging memory that written records necessarily convey to us," texts could also participate in this social dialogue over the longer term.[48] In treating written documents as a measure of reputation, we have to think carefully about the flow of information they represent.[49] While I will address the details of the sources used here at the start of each chapter, they fall into two main categories. First, a papal investigation into Charles's candidacy for sainthood generated a large collection of transcribed oral testimony (Chapter 1). Second, the rich chronicle tradition of the later Middle Ages produced numerous retellings of the Breton conflict, ranging from enthusiastic tales of knightly prowess (Chapter 2) to formal histories of the ducal dynasty (Chapter 3). The advantage of studying these narra-

46 Snaith, "Politics of Noble Reputation"; Slater, "Rumour and Reputation Management."

47 Taylor, *Virtuous Knight*, 164–65.

48 Fenster and Smail, *Fama*, 6.

49 A note, therefore, on how I have quoted my sources here: for the sake of readability and brevity, I give excerpts in English, and note the original only where the manuscript has not been edited or transcribed elsewhere. I also indicate specific words or phrases in the French or Latin (retaining the medieval spelling) where these are potentially polyvalent and/or especially significant for analysis. All source translations are my own.

tive sources is that each of them represents more than one way of looking at things. A core aim of this book is to draw attention to these fine-grained variations as a method for untangling how political culture was continually renegotiated. Comparing these different points of view, or the evolution of one point of view over time, can indicate how people established legitimacy without assuming everyone agreed on one set of rules. Conversely, because these interpretations were not entirely independent of each other, understanding why one version of a given story won out over another (or not) helps trace the ongoing political relevance of debating reputation.

My basic approach to this material owes much to two early studies of queenly reputations. Rachel Gibbons and Anne-Hélène Allirot both showed how the portrayals of certain French queens developed in distinct stages in response to both evolving political demands and specific textual traditions.[50] In Jeanne and Charles's case, I have identified three key reputational phases. Chapter 1 focuses on the first phase in 1371, when Jeanne and her family attempted to have Charles formally declared a saint following his violent death. This process of canonization, which compiled the official statements of several dozen of Jeanne and Charles's associates alongside a much wider group who claimed to have benefitted from the miracles he performed, measured Charles's (and to a lesser extent Jeanne's) leadership against the standards of both princely and clerical conduct. Chapter 2 turns to a second phase that developed from the 1380s to the 1410s, as chivalric chroniclers such as Jean Froissart and Cuvelier glorified the Breton war for their noble Anglo-French audience. Although churchmen themselves, these authors idealized martial heroism for its own sake, but the popularity of their stories also gave rise to more partisan versions.[51] Finally, Chapter 3 considers a third phase of history-writing developed under the auspices of the Montfort dukes and duchesses, which culminated in the dynastic chronicles of the later fifteenth and early sixteenth centuries. The officials who composed these texts were obviously not sympathetic to the Penthièvre cause, but they still nuanced their views of Jeanne's and Charles's place in Breton history according to the challenges facing the duchy at the end of its political independence.

The reputations developed within each phase fed both directly and indirectly into the next, but there was no overall trend across this century-and-a-half. Jeanne and Charles were by turns praised and criticized, masculin-

50 Gibbons, "Isabeau of Bavaria"; Allirot, "*Male royne boiteuse.*"

51 Cf. Smith, *War and the Making of Medieval Monastic Culture*, 3–4.

ized and feminized, compared and contrasted. Even when they agreed, these accounts of the civil war tell us little about these princes as real people, and I do not attempt to assess any extrinsic accuracy they may or may not have contained. Instead, I focus on the categories used to pass judgement on Jeanne's and Charles's conduct and characters. Each was strongly shaped by the values assigned to the other, rather than simply measured to an outside standard. This mutual influence suggests that a major consequence of joint leadership within the medieval aristocracy was that political legitimacy in times of crisis could only be fully explained and justified in relation to other actors. By revealing the spectrum of responses to co-rulership, and their uses in the face of conflict, reputation offers a new tool for understanding the visibility and effectiveness of shared power in the premodern period.

Chapter 1

SEIGNEURIAL SANCTITY

THE FIRST STAGE of Charles's reputation developed in the highly fraught circumstances almost immediately after his death, and focused on trying to make him into a canonical saint of the Catholic Church. Such haste to elevate Charles to the altars was remarkable. Even the rapidly developed cult of Saint Louis IX of France (r. 1226–1270) only obtained final approval twenty-seven years after his death on Crusade, and of the seventeen canonization processes opened in the fourteenth century, only three began more promptly than Charles's.[1] But speed was of the essence, for following the first treaty of Guérande in 1365, the position of the new Montfort dynasty within Brittany was far from secure.[2] Had Jeanne de Penthièvre and her partisans obtained papal validation of Charles's sainthood in this moment, it would have represented a serious rebound from their recent defeat. Bursts of enthusiasm for a rival's sanctity were a frequent tool of political opposition and critique in this period, while descent from "holy stock" accrued long-term status benefits to the bloodline as a whole.[3] Given the very real possibility that Jeanne or her children might revive her claim to the duchy, "Saint Charles" could help tip the balance of legitimacy in their favour.

So Charles's family and partisans swiftly promoted his veneration, centred around his tomb at Guingamp in northern Brittany.[4] The order of Franciscan friars whom Jeanne and Charles had generously patronized helped

---

1 Gaposchkin, *Making of Saint Louis*, 1–2. Of these three processes, the only one that led to canonization was that of Bridget of Sweden. Based on the data in Vauchez, *Sainteté*, 298–299, the average time to open the seventeen processes was twenty-three years after death (with a median of twelve), and the nine successful processes lasted an average of twenty-four years (median fourteen). Had Charles's canonization reached completion, it would have been the second-shortest process of the century, trailing only that of Thomas Aquinas, and the single fastest posthumous canonization, taking five years fewer than that of Pope Celestine V.

2 Jones, *Ducal Brittany*, 52–54.

3 Duch, "Chasing St Louis," esp. 330, 339, 340, 346.

4 Jones, "Politics, Sanctity and the Breton State," 221; Héry, "La 'sainteté' de Charles de Blois ou l'échec d'une entreprise," 22; Martin, *Ordres mendiants*, 407; Vauchez, "Dévotion et vie quotidienne."

spread word of his miracles both within the duchy and across France. Breton bishops even "proclaimed [Charles] a saint and martyr for justice in their sermons, [and] offered the holy sacrifice on his anniversary day, as if to a saint approved by the church."[5] Jean IV, whose relationship with the Breton elite was increasingly precarious, reacted seriously to this movement by petitioning the pope against a possible canonization in 1368; but in 1369 Pope Urban V (r. 1362–1370) accepted the request to investigate Charles's sanctity submitted by Jeanne, their daughter Marie and son-in-law Duke Louis d'Anjou, and their sons Jean and Guy de Bretagne.[6] The complicated process of canonization, which I detail further below, lasted until 1376, by which time Duke Jean had been driven into exile by his nobility, King Charles V of France was considering the annexation of the duchy, and Pope Gregory XI (r. 1370–1378) had begun relocating the papacy from Avignon in France back to Rome. Because of these political upheavals, although Charles's canonization did receive Gregory's approval and he was periodically called a saint thereafter, he was only beatified in 1904.[7]

Making the case for Charles's sanctity in this loaded context meant making sense of Charles as a saint in the midst of a devastating civil war—and one that he had lost. Previous historiography has highlighted two major narrative arcs that served this function.[8] The first was that Charles should have become a friar (or a hermit, or a bishop, or some other churchman) rather than a duke. Charles himself supposedly thought so, lamenting that he had been pulled into the war instead. His family and associates mocked this unworldliness, their scorn serving ultimately to highlight Charles's elevation above his peers. The second narrative transformed the war into a process of martyrdom, turning his defeat on earth into a spiritual victory. For many witnesses, the images of the martyred prince and would-be religious were satisfying, and they developed their accounts little beyond these basic traits. Accordingly, modern scholarship has tended to emphasize the trial as an effort to redeem a failed ruler, a pattern seen with several later medieval kings of France and England.[9]

---

5 Pocquet du Haut-Jussé, *Papes et les ducs de Bretagne*, 275.

6 Héry, "Culte de Charles de Blois," 43–50.

7 Boulet, "Canonisation de Charles de Blois"; Laurent, "Charles de Blois."

8 Vauchez, *Sainteté*, 423–24, 426–27; Cassard, "*Patience*"; Héry, "La 'sainteté' de Charles de Blois: Vertus et virtus"; Héry, "De la guerre à la paix"; cf. Klaniczay, *Holy Rulers and Blessed Princesses*, 295–97.

9 Héry, "La 'sainteté' de Charles de Blois ou l'échec d'une entreprise," 40–41; Cassard, *Guerre de succession de Bretagne*, 201; Vauchez, *Sainteté*, 187–97; Ormrod,

However, witnesses convinced of Charles's sanctity (and legitimate claim to the ducal title) would have sought evidence of holiness not just *despite* his rule, but within it. This process was not straightforward, because to be a duke, or a saint, or for that matter a man, was not a singular quality: there were multiple kinds of lordship, multiple kinds of saintliness, multiple kinds of masculinity, all offering different choices for which traits to select in a given context, and which to ignore or even subvert. The resulting narratives were not necessarily consistent, because the norms on which they were based were not. Nor could Charles's reputation be developed in isolation, for power—much like sanctity—could be exercised and evaluated only in relation to others. Accordingly, the portrayals of those around Charles were similarly reshaped to support any given characterization. As duchess, Jeanne's reputation was particularly liable to be pulled in several directions: if her feminine role as Charles's wife was a constant, her agency as his fellow lord could alternately constrain or reinforce his. Such flexibility was invaluable for constructing a positive interpretation of the recent civil war and the challenges it posed for the ideals of good lordship.

Reputation and Canonization

Late medieval processes of canonization involved creating an official collective memory, and the record we have today was produced by interactions between different participants. On one side, the proceedings were directed and shaped by ecclesiastical appointees, as the Church increasingly claimed control of the official recognition of saints.[10] The pope selected two bishops (Bayeux and Angers) and an abbot (Marmoutiers) to interrogate witnesses about Charles. They were supposed to ensure that strict legal form was followed and that no "foul play" occurred among the witnesses.[11] Meanwhile, Duchess Jeanne and her family chose the Franciscan friar Raoul de Kerguiniou as their proctor, or representative. He was responsible for assembling appropriate witnesses, and was also expected to draw up a list of "articles of interrogation." These articles normally set the questions for the papal commission to ask each witness, letting the proctor's party control the narrative surrounding their candidate. In Charles's case, though, Raoul

"Monarchy, Martyrdom, and Masculinity," 176; Elukin, "Warrior or Saint?"; Cullum, "Introduction," 5.

10 Vauchez, *Sainteté*, chap. 1; Wetzstein, "*Iura novit curia*"; Krötzl and Katajala-Peltomaa, "Approaching Twelfth- to Fifteenth-Century Miracles," 16–25.

11 Toynbee, *S. Louis of Toulouse*, 154–57.

made no list of articles to guide the trial, though the main categories of questioning were retroactively added as marginal notes.[12] Finally, three notaries recorded the testimony "in public form," summarizing in Latin the content of the question-and-answer sessions, of which three manuscript copies now survive.

On the other side, a large pool of witnesses provided the material to build the case for Charles's sanctity. From September 9 to December 18, 1371, the commissioners collected sixty individual reports concerning Charles's life and merits (*vita et meritis*), and another 139 on his miracles (*miracula*).[13] For the purposes of assessing Charles's personal reputation we are most concerned with the testimony in the *vita* section, whose sixty witnesses represented a selective social group.[14] First, they had all known Charles, so were generally of high social status, including fourteen churchmen, ten knights (four of them lords in their own right), and twelve squires. Aside from eight who had served Charles only during his childhood, the witnesses were mostly connected to the ducal entourage. All but three came from Brittany or the neighbouring northwestern provinces, and included twenty-four who had served in arms and another twenty-four who acted as administrators or attendants. Second, the witnesses generally fit the profile expected of reliable judicial testimony in this period.[15] Men were preferred to women, higher ranks to lower, and older witnesses—the average estimated age here is forty-seven years—to younger. The only *vita* witness outside this elite, male milieu was Guillemette of Saumur (a town near Angers), who with her husband had often lodged the duke and duchess over the course of fifteen years.[16] Her position as hostess still gave her privileged access to the couple and to the gossip of their servants.[17] This selectivity

12 Héry et al., eds., *Procès de canonisation*, 28.

13 Of the sixty witnesses in the first (*vita*) section of the dossier, thirty-six also gave testimony in the second.

14 Cf. Goodich, *Lives and Miracles of the Saints*, chap. 7, 297–98.

15 Katajala-Peltomaa, *Gender, Miracles, and Daily Life*, 36; Leguay and Martin, *Fastes*, 134; Everard, "Sworn Testimony," 77.

16 All references to this source use Héry et al., eds., *Procès de canonisation*: here, D29.1. For depositions (hereafter D) 1–56, the numbers cited here also correspond to those originally in Sérent, ed., *Monuments du procès*; D57–60 appear only in the new edition, and thereafter subtract 4 from the cited number if using Sérent.

17 The frequency of Charles and Jeanne's visits distinguished Guillemette from Jeanne of Candes-Saint-Martin, who after her testimony in the *miracula* section added a short account of Charles's personal conduct based on a single eight-day visit some fifteen years earlier.

in choosing witnesses was meant to produce an authoritative portrayal of Charles, not a well-rounded one. However, the group also represented the social circles where this formulation of Charles's reputation mattered most.[18]

In this context, reputation depended on a combination of convention and individual authenticity. The point of the inquiry was not to debate Charles's character, but to assemble sympathetic witnesses who could collectively provide consistent evidence for his sanctity. The template settled on in the final report focused on eight core traits discussed in most of the testimonies.[19] Charles's devotional practices such as attending Mass and spending time in prayer were mentioned by all sixty *vita* witnesses. Fifty-eight addressed his personal character, especially his humility and kindness, as well as his charity to the poor and the Church. His striking regime of ascetic penance appeared in fifty-seven accounts, followed by his chastity (fifty-two) and sobriety (fifty-one). Finally, his patience in the face of adversity (forty-seven) and his commitment to justice (forty-six) rounded out the list, lagging behind mainly because witnesses who had known Charles only as a child were mostly silent on traits from his ducal career. Within each category, the notaries relied heavily on stock phrases to make it obvious how the testimony substantiated accepted ideas of piety, generosity, temperance, and so on. This formulaic repetition largely obscured the personal voices of individual witnesses.

Nevertheless, this broad consensus left room for variety in the specifics of each deposition. Unlike hostile interrogations where questioner and witness were in opposition—Joan of Arc's trial being a notorious, and well-studied, example—Charles's trial was less strictly managed, even than other canonization processes.[20] Virtually no two witnesses addressed the main themes in the same order, which let them recombine these elements in different ways. More importantly, witnesses could apparently elaborate as they saw fit, perhaps reflecting their status as respectable individuals. The commissioners seem to have preferred open-ended questions, asking simply how the witness knew Charles was patient, or just, or humble, then following up only where they felt additional clarification was needed. They gave witnesses opportunities to enrich their own narratives, but did not challenge them.

---

18 Cf. Goodich, *Lives and Miracles of the Saints*, chap. 7, 295.

19 The numbers listed here reflect the categorizations in the manuscript margins, and may slightly underrepresent the actual mentions of the topic in the testimony.

20 Flannery and Walter, *Culture of Inquisition*; Sullivan, *Interrogation*; Hobbins, *Trial*; Vauchez, *Sainteté*, 650; Toynbee, *S. Louis of Toulouse*, 166.

This conversational space kept the concrete evidence for Charles's sanctity rooted in each witness's own experience and reflected their access to information. Even within the restricted milieu of the ducal court, there was real variation based on one's exact position and relationships. When questioned on a detail of Charles's prayers, for example, the courtier Baudet de la Folie protested that "he does not know because he is not a cleric."[21] Meanwhile, Charles's manservant Jean Forestier confirmed the duke's chastity on the grounds that he himself had been present in the bedroom almost every night.[22] Many of the witnesses knew each other, of course, and so during the trial they confirmed one another's testimony or reported hearsay from around the princely household (even, on occasion, from Charles's private confessors).[23] It is particularly useful that we can compare and contrast different retellings of the same experiences to better understand how witnesses reinterpreted these events when moving them from personal memory to public record.

Still, the process of curating and constructing Charles's reputation began long before 1371. The princely couple themselves had helped circulate relevant information. Jeanne, for instance, told one squire that Charles's austerities had increased since his return from England.[24] Charles helped sow the seeds of his own later martyrdom narrative when he spoke "to the people in the house of the Friars Preacher [of Nantes] and explain[ed] to them what he had had to undergo in his prison."[25] Even attempting to hide many of his pious acts only helped fan the flames: as court gossip called attention to his virtue, it became all the more admirable for being originally hidden.[26] Already during Charles's lifetime, a combination of deliberate interactions and incidental social pressures established patterns of information about him.

It is therefore essential not to mistake either concrete details or general consensus in this testimony for straightforward fact. Historians such as Jean-Christophe Cassard have tried to assess how Charles's companions

---

21 D5.5.

22 D51.6.

23 D34.4.

24 D21.9.

25 D18.3.

26 E.g., D11.3, 18.5, 22.13, 35.8, 31.10, 37.4, 93.7. See also Lochrie, *Covert Operations*, 4; Constable, "Attitudes Toward Self-Inflicted Suffering," 21; Guay, "Émotions," 40–42, 45, 48–49.

really felt about the duke, or what Charles was actually like.[27] But these are not productive questions as we have no real evidence one way or another. The canonization process was a performance, not a confession. Witnesses chose to recollect some events and not others. Their reactions, both positive and negative, were not necessarily what they had been at the time, but the ones useful in the present context. What we can analyze are the decisions they made in adapting their material: what information was important, and what did it mean? The feedback loop between the expectations of canonization and witnesses' memories produced a composite picture rather than a seamless whole, showing how Charles's reputation(s) consolidated both on an individual level and within a courtly environment.

Jeanne's reputation here is, if anything, even more complicated than Charles's. André Vauchez has suggested that neither the witnesses nor their interrogators were interested in Charles's family life.[28] Still, given that Jeanne was not the main focus, it is significant that three-quarters of the *vita* witnesses made at least passing reference to her, usually as Charles's wife. While they were here to talk about Charles, most witnesses had lived with their princes as a couple, and knew Jeanne as well as, and in a few cases even better than, her husband.[29] Several remained in her service in 1371, and she may have even encouraged them to attend. This contact cut across all aspects of the ducal court, which meant most notably that Charles's companions in arms were Jeanne's associates as well. Yet personal connections alone were not enough to explain mentions of the duchess at Angers. Some of Jeanne's long-time retainers, such as the priest Guillaume Bérengier or the marshal Alain Maréchal, did not bring her into their testimony.[30] Instead, Jeanne served as a deliberate counterpoint to Charles. When and why she mattered were defined by his reputation, rather than on her own terms—though Jeanne's perceived comparative value was not set in stone.

At the same time, her presence (even implicit) meant that Charles's own reputation also operated within a framework of shared power, which presented both challenges and opportunities for constructing his sanctity. The first eight witnesses, for example, had known Charles up until his marriage, while eleven others had known him from that point onwards, so they used

27 Cassard, "Coulisses" (cf. Vauchez, *Sainteté*, 424); Cassard, *Charles de Blois*.

28 Vauchez, *Sainteté*, 422.

29 Graham-Goering, *Princely Power*, 149–53.

30 D19.2, 45.1.

this union to contextualize their testimony.[31] This approach underscored the contingent nature of Charles's authority—it was Jeanne who made him a duke. The connection between his marriage and his status could even be made explicit: "he entered into marriage with the lady duchess of Brittany, and went off to rule the said duchy," or "he was married to the lady Jeanne of Brittany, then countess of Penthièvre and afterwards duchess of Brittany, and he had possession of the said duchy."[32] Given the prevalence of heiresses among the medieval aristocracy, the fact that Charles's title derived from his position as Jeanne's spouse would have been routine. Katrin Sjursen has pointed out the limitations of understanding medieval noblewomen primarily through their life stages (daughter, wife, mother, widow) rather than by the actions they took, and indeed, witnesses' references to Jeanne's role said little about her as an individual.[33] But it mattered that *Charles* had a wife, and I suggest that we should consider the impact of the matrimonial cycle on noblemen more than has often been the case.

Lordly Responsibilities and Civil War

If this process of canonization cobbled together one possible saintly template, it also had to grapple with the complex expectations associated with being a duke. After all, *dominium* worked on a sliding scale: good lordship on earth reflected divine lordship above.[34] But there were latent tensions inherent to the responsibilities of secular lordship. On one hand, a lord should provide effective (military) leadership, rewarding their followers and bringing them victories and wealth. On the other, they were also supposed to protect their dependents, especially women, children, and priests; and more broadly promote the common good. Normally, these commitments should not have interfered with each other, but during a civil war, they became almost mutually exclusive. The witnesses used two main strategies to navigate this contradiction and so bolster Charles's seigneurial and saintly legitimacy across this period of intensified conflict.

First, Charles had to be absolved of responsibility for the violence damaging his duchy while retaining his capacity for good military leadership. Second, proving his commitment to the welfare of his people could mitigate

31 Cf. Graham-Goering, *Princely Power*, 149–53.

32 D5.11, D52.2.

33 Sjursen, "Pirate, Traitor, Wife," 153.

34 Van Engen, "Sacred Sanctions"; Davies, *Lords and Lordship*, 16.

or even cancel out the consequences of the war. Both approaches relied on seeing Charles's authority not in autocratic terms, but as part of a larger system of power. Willingness to listen to counsel, both human and divine, was considered essential to good lordship, but it was also necessary to ignore bad advice: the stock figure of the prince misled by wicked councillors was a mainstay of discussions of just rule in this period. Charles's relationships with those around him allowed witnesses to align his priorities to the highest standards of lordship, ultimately idealizing his reign as it ought to have been.

To show how tensions between the two primary responsibilities of lordship played out in the canonization trial, I take as my starting-point Charles's victory at the siege of Quimper. Very few detailed military actions came up during the canonization trial, aside from the battle of Auray where Charles achieved supposed martyrdom. In defeat, the devastation of his duchy was just one of the many sufferings inflicted upon him. But in victory, Charles rather than his enemies became responsible for the violence, and that meant his actions had to be legitimate.

Quimper, a town in western Brittany, and especially its bishop Alain An Gall, had favoured the Montfortists since the early days of the war, but Charles besieged it in March 1344 and captured it by assault on May 1.[35] While siege warfare was a staple of the Anglo-French conflicts in this period and condoned a range of unusually violent acts, what happened at Quimper apparently surprised contemporaries.[36] A near-contemporary Latin chronicle, the *Chronicon Britannicum*, reported that in the sack of the city

> there were killed by him fourteen hundred people, nor did Charles cease from the said cruelty and slaughter until it was announced to him that a certain infant was nursing at the breasts of its slain mother. Hearing this made him break off from this slaughter, and because of this cruelty a great scandal arose in Brittany, and especially in Cornouaille [the region of Quimper].[37]

This account may have exaggerated, but its accusations likely had some real grounding in the communal memory to which the chronicler alluded. Indeed, rumours circulated that Charles had been "a bad man, a pillager and plunderer."[38] The brutality of lords and knights was a constant social and moral concern in this period. This episode of violence showed how easy it

35 Sumption, *Trial by Battle*, 434.

36 Taylor, *Chivalry and the Ideals of Knighthood*, 211–12.

37 Morice, ed., *Mémoires*, 1:7–8.

38 D128.1.

was, when tensions built into civil war, to tip over the line between licit violence and excessive cruelty, which was associated with tyranny. A contemporary chronicler, recalling a similar sack by the Black Prince in 1370, even described the three thousand dead inhabitants as martyrs and marvelled at how a prince could not have taken pity on such innocents.[39] In this light, the shocking image of the dead woman and helpless baby in the *Chronicon Britannicum* was no coincidence. It undercut Charles's legitimacy as duke of Brittany by suggesting he acted un-ducally, inflicting violence where he should have extended his protection.

The nine witnesses who discussed Quimper were well aware of what had happened and its implications for Charles's reputation as a good lord. Seven said they had been present at the siege and the remaining two were likely to have been. Six had served in arms, while two were priests and one was Charles's servant; those who had not been with Charles's own contingent relied on what they had seen and heard in the aftermath. As active participants themselves, they might have believed that rebellion against one's lawful lord meant forfeiting any claim to safety. But in their testimony, only two of them noted the presence of *rebelles* in Quimper.[40] Rather than a story of a rebellion justly put down, most witnesses foregrounded a war against external invaders. Quimper was in the hands of generic enemies or specifically the English, and Charles used force to capture these foes.[41] This framing highlighted the temporary nature of the situation, delegitimizing the occupiers and suggesting that Charles was really coming to the defence of his town. By giving the duke a more specific and unambiguously legitimate target for his violence, they sidestepped the grey area of civil conflict.

Moreover, the witnesses turned the siege into positive evidence that Charles fulfilled the expectations of military lordship by justifying the city's capture as a miraculous intervention. This approach made Charles not just an effective war leader, protecting his troops and ensuring their success in battle, but a divinely sanctioned one. Crucially, this leadership did not rely on the personal performance of violence, as was usual for a knight and a lord. Instead, it was God who came to Charles's assistance, making his victory a manifestation of the divine order.

---

39 Froissart, *Chroniques*, ed. Luce, 7:250.

40 D38.12, 40.10. Cf. Gauvard, "Révoltes," 55–56.

41 D38.12, 40.10, 41.10, 147.8, 149.7, 152.2–3, 152.6–7, 153.3.

In the first miracle, Charles was alerted to a spy on the eve of battle.[42] This spy was "a poor little woman" who feigned weakness, and Charles had previously pitied and fed her—obviously fulfilling his lordly responsibility towards the vulnerable. Then, on the critical night, it was divinely revealed to Charles that she had gone to expose the situation of his army to "our enemies" in Quimper. Caught upon her return, she confessed to regularly trading information for gold, which was discovered in her hut. Charles was able to issue precise instructions to his men to keep the situation under control. At the same time (the witness believed) he was inspired by no human intervention, but purely by the advice he received from above, giving his leadership the edge of divine favour.

Later, all nine witnesses attested that the tides themselves ceased to rise at their usual hour when Quimper was taken, protecting Charles's men as they attacked the city from the estuary and giving them time to carry the day.[43] In all but three reports, Charles deliberately sought the miracle through his prayers, and two witnesses claimed this interpretation was widespread among the local inhabitants and sailors.[44] The ability to request a miracle was a valuable characteristic in a war leader, one that even let Charles achieve a difficult military victory without lifting a weapon himself. Charles's arms-bearer, who accompanied him during the attack, reported that "for as long as the assault lasted, Charles prayed with joined hands towards the east."[45] One of Charles's priests heard from some knights that while his men stormed the town, the duke himself "withdrew to the side and on bent knees made a prayer to God for the sake of his undertaking." The tide held and "at the time when Charles made his prayer, his men entered the town through a well-fortified point and captured the town and the enemies." A third witness had been present in the retinue of Olivier de Tinténiac, a nobleman related to Duchess Jeanne by marriage.[46] Seeing the assault threatened by the impending tide, Charles withdrew to a private space. The duke was dressed for battle, but with Olivier's help removed the armour from his arms and legs. He knelt on a stone and prayed with raised hands that Christ would stem the tide to let them proceed. Only after this secret

42 D152.2–3.

43 D41.10, 46.12, 147.8, 148.10, 149.7, 150.17, 151.7, 152.5–8, 153.3.

44 D46.12, 150.17.

45 D151.7.

46 D152.6–7; Jones, ed., *Recueil des actes de Charles de Blois et Jeanne de Penthièvre*, no. 16.

ritual did Charles have his men capture the city. These visual details are striking: the joined hands, bent knees, and deliberate removal of his equipment all emphasized that Charles was not acting as a knight. Stripping away his masculine warrior persona tacitly exonerated Charles from any violence committed against his people in Quimper, while proving that his divinely empowered lordship brought his men safely to victory over the enemy.

The success of Charles's strategy here also proved his superiority to those who normally advised him. A squire who had known Charles since childhood reported that the duke had argued with his knights and barons, who wanted to attack somewhere other than the tidal flood zone.[47] Charles replied that since they had chosen their spot, they would not change it; by God's grace the sea would not harm them. The miraculous vindication of his unconventional tactic underscored his extraordinary leadership: he was right where others had been wrong, discerning enough to trust to God rather than to mere men, and backed by divine intervention on his army's behalf. On more mundane occasions, too, Charles's disagreement with his counsellors could enhance his aura as a military commander. At the fateful battle of Auray, the knight Geoffroy de Dinan claimed a treaty was proposed whereby the Breton people would pay thirty thousand *livres* to the Montfortists across five years.[48] Several of Charles's nobles supported the offer, preferring taxation to combat; but Charles declared that rather than further burdening his subjects, he would rather fight for them. Charles's willingness to put his own life on the line compared favourably with the reluctance (even cowardice?) of his advisors. It also justified his death not only as martyrdom but as a commitment to his obligations as a lord, though here battle was to the advantage of the people rather than their detriment. Because Charles's ability to pursue the war in exemplary fashion could not be taken for granted, his decisions were instead explained with reference to other influences, either inspiration from above or the rejection of lesser ideals. These associations linked Charles's military leadership to his position as a saint, standing between the human and the divine.

The backdrop of conflict remained problematic at the canonization, however, as seen in how the witnesses approached the other side of lordship. Since the war by its nature disrupted the way things ought to be, it threatened Charles's ability to maintain public order. Only three of the nine witnesses at Quimper—Charles's arms-bearer and two other squires—

47 D41.10.

48 D56.8.

attempted to address the aftermath of the siege directly. Their testimony focused on Charles's safeguarding of the Church during the assault, a theme with particular resonance within Brittany as one of the so-called regalian (sovereign) rights claimed by its dukes.[49] The fortified town was divided in half by the river Steïr, with the area to the east under the jurisdiction of the bishop and cathedral chapter, and to the west under that of the duke.[50] Having breached the walls, Charles allegedly made straight for the cathedral, where he gathered together all the local clergy and placed them, and the relics and ornaments of the churches, under his protection. In so doing, he contrasted with his foes, who did not hesitate to capture, despoil, and even kill priests from the other side. Moreover, Charles's advisors suggested that since the town was too large to hold easily, the duke should destroy the bishop's portion. Charles refused, for love of the Church or so as not to displease God, and instead ordered his own walls dismantled.[51] This decision had no actual military repercussions, as Quimper remained loyal thereafter.[52] In the moment, however, it clearly showcased Charles's seigneurial priorities.

This episode offered a different reading of lordship than in the miracle stories. By attending to the Church in person, Charles was again dissociated from the violence happening elsewhere, just as he had stood aside to pray for divine intervention. Now, though, being a good lord meant working against his own men and interests rather than on their behalf, as he had done during the assault. The witnesses variously provided this anecdote as evidence for Charles's commitment to justice or his acts of charity (what the compilers of the testimony later categorized as "mercy and almsgiving"). It therefore showcased Charles's lordship as a matter of promoting order and championing the common good.

Although this theme was only partially developed among the Quimper witnesses, it was more successfully demonstrated in other contexts. Historians have noted the sporadic attempts in the *vita* testimony to cast Charles as a peacemaker. Direct references to his continuous prayers for peace and ability to settle disputes complemented more oblique suggestions of reconciliation through the miraculous conversion of Englishmen and Montfortist

49 Graham-Goering, *Princely Power*, 229.

50 Leguay, *Réseau urbain*, 304.

51 D38.12, 40.10, 49.10.

52 Jean de Montfort would die of illness following a disastrous attempt to retake the city the following year (Sumption, *Trial by Battle*, 471), and it was besieged again by the young Jean de Montfort in November 1364 even after Charles himself was dead (Jones, ed., *Recueil des actes de Jean IV*, no. 41).

partisans to Charles's cult following his death.[53] But given that Charles had manifestly *not* brought peace in his lifetime, his peacemaking is better understood as a separation between the responsibilities of lordship that allowed Charles to concentrate only on his duchy's welfare while outsourcing the rest. Here, the mechanics of counsel were particularly effective for dissociating him from violence and, indeed, downplaying the overall importance of the war in understanding his rule.

Charles's manservant Jean Gauvin, for instance, recalled the duke's complaint that

> "I am dressed in cloths of gold and silks, [but] I would truly prefer to be dressed in lesser cloths in the manner of the Friars Minor, and except that it would displease my people, truly I would clothe myself with other, simpler cloths; and I believe it would have been best if I had been a Franciscan when I was made duke, for the people of Brittany cannot be at peace because of the discord existing between me and my adversary, and I can do nothing about it save by the counsel of the barons and others of my duchy."[54]

From this perspective, Charles undertook his princely career out of external obligation rather than personal interest. He had a duty to the Breton people, on whose behalf he lived up to his role. At the same time, the ongoing war harmed these same people, so Charles's priorities had to align with theirs.[55] Instead, those around Charles became responsible for prolonging the conflict. This dichotomy between Charles and his entourage ensured that both sides of lordship were addressed, while letting Charles close the gap between his idealized and actual rule.[56]

Lest his lordship be perceived as unstable, witnesses normally reported that Charles was able to work closely with his council. This harmonious relationship underpinned his love of justice, and so served his reputation as an effective ruler. He appointed the best councillors he could, and they in turn ensured that his seneschals, officers, and other ministers of justice were competent.[57] Moreover, he supervised the council, making sure that they debated matters in a timely manner and reprimanding them when they sought to obstruct petitions or allowed a case to drag on.[58] This dynamic

53 D9.2, 15.9, 26.3, 35.4; D50.1–5, 132.5, 143.3–4, 144.4–5, 150.9–10, 150.13–14.

54 D31.8.

55 Cf. D13.3, 26.3, 39.8, 55.3.

56 Cf. Plassmann, "William of Malmesbury," 2–4.

57 D12.13, 19.11, 23.13, 24.9, 28.11, 31.11, 34.11, 40.9, 46.10.

58 D27.2, 21.2, 31.11.

exemplified good leadership, soliciting well-informed input while ultimately taking command. By stressing both reciprocity and authority, this model reflected contemporary conceptions of governance.[59] Accordingly, a gentleman in the service of Jeanne's uncle-by-marriage Hervé de Léon, reported that Charles governed the duchy of Brittany by Hervé's council, while a squire spoke of the council's role in ensuring the just administration of the duchy.[60] Conforming to the latest expectations of public order management was an attribute of good lordship, and perhaps doubly so in what might otherwise have been seen first as a period of disorder.

However, the management of the war, even off the battlefield, provoked differences of opinion. While armies in the fourteenth-century kingdom of France still relied on the obligations of military service from their noble fiefholders, these were generally insufficient to the needs of prolonged campaigns and had to be supplemented with wages and the hiring of paid troops—the etymological definition of "soldiers." The issue of how Charles spent his money was discussed by a number of witnesses, generally under the headings of mercy or piety (donations to churches) and generosity or alms (charity towards the poor, especially giving money and food). These were all acts expected of someone in Charles's position, as part of the obligations of care for the weak. Indeed, we may suspect that his benefaction might have gone relatively unremarked in more peaceful circumstances, where it might have lived up to the practices of conspicuous giving expected of elite men.

As it was, however, Charles's desire to look after ordinary Bretons clashed with the financial demands of the war, and so Charles clashed with his companions. Charles's almsgiving provoked recriminations from his council.[61] A knight, a servant, and a priest all noted that Charles was always willing to take the side of the Church against his own officers and advisors, just as had happened with the walls of Quimper.[62] One squire's brother had brought the duke a thousand florins from Charles's captain of Morlaix (a castle and town in northwestern Brittany). Charles instructed his chancellor to take charge of them but not breathe a word of the money's existence, "because if my paid men-at-arms should know that I had that money, they

59 Genet, "Government," 12–13.

60 D11.2, 48.10.

61 D11.4.

62 D12.11, 24.5, 35.12.

would seek it of me, and so I would not have anything to spend on the poor."[63] Charles was expected to reward those who fought for him, but he chose to prioritize his other responsibilities when the funds were limited.[64] Similarly, Charles's household administrators complained that the duke spent all he could on the Church and the poor, instead of on his war efforts.[65] And Charles's treasurer Pierre Poulard among others remonstrated with Charles to levy the taxes needed to fund the war and maintain a lifestyle appropriate to his rank. Instead, out of compassion for his subjects, Charles preferred to borrow money from the pope, the king of France, and other great lords, with his duchy as collateral.[66] Other witnesses, such as the ducal secretary Guillaume André, recalled giving similar loans themselves.[67] Charles here made use of his followers and allies to fulfill his obligations to his subjects, rather than using his subjects to supply the needs of his men. By reporting explicit debate on which of Charles's ducal responsibilities came first, the witnesses were able to parcel them out: the pursuit of the war was displaced onto Charles's entourage, whereas he remained concerned with the business of peace.

At its extreme, this distinction could suggest that Charles ruled *beyond* the war. The squire Henri Le Prévôt explained how Charles's council (to which he himself belonged) tried to impose taxes "for the defence of the homeland [*patria*]." Here, the council saw the taxes as contributing to the protection of the duchy against external invaders. But these efforts were undercut by the duke himself, who "always wished that his subjects should live peacefully under him."[68] It was not until much later in the Hundred Years' War that the idea of permanent taxation developed; at this point, taxes were still seen as emergency funds and were expected to cease when the immediate need was over. By objecting to the levy, Charles indicated that the problem was not the tax itself, but that it prolonged the undesirable conflict. His opposition to taxation implied that he ought to be able to rule as a lord in peacetime rather than in war.

---

63 D16.5.

64 Ironically, unreliable pay drove soldiers to live off the local peasantry instead: Taylor, *Chivalry and the Ideals of Knighthood*, 228.

65 D38.7; cf. 35.10.

66 D49.3.

67 D28.4; cf. 23.5, 38.4, 45.4.

68 D49.4.

Accordingly, witnesses emphasized Charles's efforts to create a semblance of normalcy. The extreme generosity that frustrated his council in fact served to ensure good lordship continued under extenuating circumstances. Charles rebuilt a Dominican priory "which had been practically destroyed and consumed by the wars," a church and tower that were ruined, and paupers' homes that had been burned.[69] He also had a new hospital built within the walls of Guingamp (in northern Brittany, one of his main residences) when it became unsafe to reach the original extramural hospital.[70] Such activities were effectively retroactive extensions of the safeguard he pre-emptively extended to the churches of Quimper. Unlike the siege, however, these pious donations had the merit of avoiding the question of whose army it was that had caused the damage originally.[71] Done right, the exercise of good lordship in the sense of maintaining order could substitute for failures of military lordship.

Going one step further, the preservation of good rule could, like Charles's battlefield leadership, operate on a miraculous level. A squire at Quimper claimed that

> although the grains had been cut around the said town by the people of the army of the said Lord Charles, nevertheless the residents of that land harvested grain more abundantly in those places the following August than they would have if it had not been thus cut and eradicated.[72]

He credited this report to local residents and farmers, adding that it was well known that "such bounties had not arisen in the region of Brittany since his [Charles's] death as they had done during his life." Claiming that the violence of Charles's army resulted, through his lordship, in such a positive outcome was a remarkable attempt to make Quimper almost a victimless siege. Another squire likewise insisted that Charles's rule materially benefited his people:

> It is commonly said by the populace of the homeland of Brittany that the people of the duchy of Brittany, during the lifetime of the said Lord Charles, had greater abundance of crops and of all other goods, and were richer in material possessions, although they were beleaguered by the wars, than they were after his death.[73]

69 D11.4, 12.9, 18.7, 34.7, 39.7, 42.8, 49.9.

70 D44.6.

71 Tellingly, some witnesses who might have brought up Charles's safeguard after the siege, such as Pierre Martin, a Franciscan of Quimper, did not (D33).

72 D150.18.

73 D48.11; cf. 132.4.

Reconciling crisis and stability was a powerful tool for enhancing Charles's legitimacy by suggesting that the war had ultimately been unable to disrupt his tenure as duke. Elevating him above the conflict restored him to what he should have been, especially in light of his still-recent defeat. A key response to a period of heightened tension was to double down on the status quo. Indeed, the political aims of the canonization effort itself may be read in this vein, promoting Charles's uninterrupted lordship even beyond the end of his mortal life.

Witnesses' efforts to navigate between the different responsibilities of lordship nuance our understanding of how canonization reconfigured a ruler's reputation. For some, sanctity might have been a way to make up for "martial failings," retconning past disappointments into vindications of virtue.[74] But leaving it there oversimplifies the *co*-construction of sainthood and lordship: Charles's seigneurial successes were just as integral to interpreting his holiness. Because the civil war made it hard to cast his authority in unambiguously positive terms, witnesses instead stressed how Charles lived up to different aspects of lordship in different contexts, covering all the bases but not all at once. At the same time, the exceptionality demanded of saints meant Charles had to defy ordinary expectations, so we should be cautious about seeing disagreements about tactics or policy just as lapses of lordship retrospectively papered over. Instead, a useful modern analogy might be the maverick action hero whose offbeat decisions provoke skepticism then admiration (a perennial audience favourite). Charles's clashes with those around him were an easy way for witnesses to make him stand out.

Such interpretations were made easier by the fact that lordship was already understood not in isolation or absolutely, but contingently. A lord's practical ability to use counsel wisely also had an extended moral significance for evaluating and communicating their authority. In the canonization inquiry, reputation was therefore inevitably established by situating Charles within a wider framework of spiritual and earthly relationships. Moreover, the associative process of lordship made it possible to shift the impetus for violence away from Charles himself.[75] It became God's responsibility where justified, and that of ordinary barons where it fell short of the ideal. Charles's reputation thus appeared in its best light when compared to others and when his lordship was framed collectively.

---

74 Elukin, "Warrior or Saint?," 194; cf. Lewis, *Kingship and Masculinity*, 57.

75 Cf. Hardy, *Associative Political Culture*.

Gender and Aristocratic Partnerships

The version of Charles's leadership that rose above the war tended to foreground what Mark Ormrod has called the "feminized" aspects of rulership, such as peacemaking, intercession, and compassion, which under more usual circumstances could readily be outsourced to a male ruler's spouse.[76] Meanwhile, other witnesses inverted Charles's authority to enhance his spiritual standing. Although this approach might first seem to come at the expense of his secular role, it ultimately preserved his masculine reputation as a knight and lord. Jeanne's presence as his wife and duchess contributed both passively and actively to this process. As with Charles, however, the parameters of her gender and authority were not fixed, but depended on their position within a shared framework.

The portrayal of Charles's piety as far outside the princely norm has often been taken as straightforward evidence for his lack of leadership ability. A recurring trope among Charles's associates and attendants (and sometimes even his priests) was their boredom and impatience with his lengthy masses, prayers, and discussions of saints' lives.[77] Witnesses suggested this behaviour was inappropriate for a prince in his position, and even ridiculed him for it. Michel Barbelot, the duke's barber, recalled a particularly sharp contrast when Charles would humble himself before the poor "to such an extent that certain nobles who saw it derided him, saying, 'You see our duke, certainly he would humble himself more before some old woman than before one good man-at-arms.'"[78] Charles himself reportedly acknowledged this contradiction, as we saw above in his lament for his unrealized career as a Franciscan monk. Moreover, this clash of purpose was fundamentally due to Jeanne. Michel further recalled the duke's claim that if not for his wife and sons, and the defence of his rights in the duchy, he would have entered the Carthusian order of monks.[79] Jeanne's presence motivated his pursuit of the war, making his martial functions an outgrowth of his marital relationship. These and many similar claims suggested a dichotomy between being a good duke and leading a religious life.

But the reluctant duke was a convenient narrative for the purposes of canonization, as truly exceptional piety was an obvious asset to Charles's

---

76 Ormrod, "Monarchy, Martyrdom, and Masculinity," 175.

77 E.g., D19.6, 24.2, 35.7, 37.3, 40.5, 41.5, 47.4, 56.4.

78 D47.2.

79 D47.4.

case whether founded in reality or not. There are abundant indications even in the testimony that Charles's devotional routine had not actually greatly interfered with his pursuit of ordinary business, as he would interrupt it in the company of important guests, in order to travel, and to see to other pressing affairs, including the war.[80] This habit resulted in something of a nesting doll effect, where Charles maintained the outward appearance of a prince, conforming to the expectations of his station, while privately expressing a supposedly secret piety.

Charles could achieve the best of both worlds because how far they were actually in contradiction is debatable. If covert spiritual virtue ostensibly contrasted with the visibility of knightly exploits, the two were ultimately both validated by having an external audience.[81] Saint Louis, France's most respected king, had undertaken similar acts of humility both in imitation of Christ and as an exemplar of good kingship, so this well-recognized theme need not have implied negative repercussions for Charles's princely image.[82] Parallels between secular warriors and monks as "soldiers of Christ" were recognized early in the Christian tradition.[83] And although the line between secular and clerical masculinities was constantly evolving, the demands of manhood placed on both monks and rulers overlapped in relying heavily on an assumption of control.[84] Between the eleventh and thirteenth centuries, substantial Church reform and the emergence of a new knightly aristocracy had jointly tended to focus pressure on the issues of chastity and violence. The former entailed mastery of one's own body, though this expectation could clash with that of exerting sexual dominance over others. The latter stressed physical strength exercised with discipline and restraint. If men of the cloth and of the sword might manifest these requirements in different ways, their gender rested on parallel foundations.[85] At the canonization, then, it was both necessary to heighten the contrast between the two frame-

80 E.g., D9.10, 12.3, 15.7, 18.13, 19.4, 22.10, 23.10, 33.3, 46.3, 51.2, 57.2, 58.6.

81 Taylor, *Chivalry and the Ideals of Knighthood*, 64–65.

82 Gaposchkin, *Making of Saint Louis*, 106–7; cf. Lewis, *Kingship and Masculinity*, 149, 202.

83 Vauchez, "Notion de *miles Christi*."

84 Armstrong-Partida, "Sex and Priestly Masculinity"; Thibodeaux, *Manly Priest*; Aurell, "Rapport introductif"; Smith, "Saints in Shining Armor"; Nelson, "Monks, Secular Men and Masculinity"; McNamara, "*Herrenfrage*."

85 Karras, *From Boys to Men*, 24; Smith, *War and the Making of Medieval Monastic Culture*, 43–44, 50.

works and possible to use Charles's religious persona to lay the groundwork for his ducal one.

Many of the standard characteristics recurring across the witness testimony highlighted Charles's masculine self-control. After all, contemporary manuals of rulership admonished, how could a man expect to govern others if he could not govern himself?[86] The evidence that Charles met this criterion included abundant reports of his restrained reactions to news of both victory and defeat, as well as his tolerant attitude towards those who showed him disrespect. Far from signs of apathy or meekness that might have demoralized his followers, such equanimity attested Charles's strength of will and the superior discipline which marked the best of the nobility.[87] The same behaviour which contributed to his saintly reputation for humility here would have enhanced his reputation as a *prudhomme*, a worthy man, in courtly circles.

But some forms of discipline posed different problems for noblemen than for churchmen. For aristocratic and clerical men alike, chastity was considered a form of battle, epitomizing self-mastery; but taken too far it was dangerous in a male ruler, who also had a duty to perpetuate his lineage.[88] At the same time, elite laymen could be considered unmanly if they indulged too freely in sex, either hetero- or homosexual.[89] The solution here was to focus on Charles's conformity to the standards of continent marriage, an increasingly popular theme in saints' lives of this period, and it was in this context that witnesses most regularly mentioned Jeanne.[90] Discussions of Charles's chastity repeatedly confirmed that he had "never known carnally any woman save his wife." Jeanne's presence in this role made Charles a successful father—four of their six children were explicitly mentioned during the trial—and well-behaved spouse, allowing him to reconcile bodily control and sexual purity with the obligations of a dynastic prince and a man.[91] She was therefore cast as a necessary component of his masculine authority in this contested space. Her contribution here was passive and impersonal;

86 Lewis, *Kingship and Masculinity*, 2, 26–27; cf. Cassard, "*Patience*," 290.

87 Taylor, "Chivalric Conversation," 178–79.

88 Cullum, "Introduction," 4–5; Thibodeaux, *Manly Priest*, 38, 124; Bagerius and Ekholst, "Unruly Queen," 108.

89 Ormrod, "Sexualities of Edward II"; Karras and Pierpont, *Sexuality in Medieval Europe*, 200.

90 Weissenberg, "Sacrament of Marriage."

91 D9.5, 12.5, 24.1; Karras, *From Boys to Men*, 16, 43; McNamara, "*Herrenfrage*," 5.

even her name and title were rarely used. Nevertheless, Charles's performance of masculinity in turn confirmed *a priori* Jeanne's own ability to fulfill the requirements of a wife and mother.

Chastity was generally the least detailed of Charles's virtues (after all, it was fundamentally an absence of behaviour rather than its presence), but such regular mentions confirmed the importance of the spouses' "marital community" as part of Charles's (and by extensions, Jeanne's) reputations.[92] Repeating this rather bland trope was, moreover, only one option for showing how their roles fit together. One of Charles's manservants put a different spin on the dynamic of chastity by bringing in the idea of conjugal debt, where both spouses owed each other sex: the duke claimed that were he not obliged to by the marriage vows, he would not sleep with his wife at all.[93] This approach was again meant to satisfy two competing demands. Charles's status meant he could not enjoy the spiritually purer states of virginity or a celibate marriage, but at least he had *wanted* such a lifestyle.[94] If, meanwhile, a complete lack of desire for women might be unknightly, Charles had already come out on top in the competition for women via his high-status marriage.[95] As part of this balancing act, Jeanne remained passive, but she now interrupted Charles's spiritual aspirations. Their identities were still paired, but as counterparts rather than reinforcements.

The external mediation of Charles's piety was also a running theme in the more dramatic demonstrations of his personal discipline such as his sobriety, his penances, and the adversities he bore, which ranged from the commonplace to the extreme. On a day-to-day level, he might fast, or eat and drink only a little simple food. Increasingly, he tied knotted cords tightly around his torso, wore a rough hairshirt (*cilicium*) against his skin, slept without a mattress, and embraced other similar inflictions. Finally, he performed individual feats of pious endurance, most notably a barefoot pilgrimage in winter from La Roche-Derrien to Tréguier, about six kilometres apart. These practices had clear and deliberate associations with clerical asceticism, and especially Franciscan traditions of penance. The knotted cords in particular were described as being "in the likeness of the Friars Minor."[96]

92 Weissenberg, "Sacrament of Marriage," 463.

93 D10.5; Brundage, *Law, Sex, and Christian Society*, 241–42.

94 See Thibodeaux, *Manly Priest*, chap. 1; McGlynn and Moll, "Chaste Marriage"; cf. Weissenberg, "Sacrament of Marriage," 462, 464, 467; McNamara, "*Herrenfrage*," 10.

95 Karras, *From Boys to Men*, 51, 54, 56.

96 D10.9, 27.7.

They also aligned Charles with recent saintly models, most notably his relative Saint Louis, who also wore a hairshirt, but also Saint Yves, a Breton jurist saint whose canonization Charles had personally sponsored and whose garment he was said to have worn over the hairshirt.[97] This emulation was as close as Charles could effectively come to realizing his religious calling, and so helped substantiate the sincerity of his aspiration while performing masculine feats of endurance.[98]

However, these devotions interacted with the physical demands of Charles's ducal position in complex ways. For some witnesses, it was important to mitigate the consequences of these rigours to show that Charles remained up to his worldly responsibilities. They tempered their accounts of Charles's asceticism with evidence that he was able—perhaps with some encouragement—to take sufficient care of his body. His physicians' nagging on the matter of fasting apparently succeeded in preventing Charles from going overboard, ultimately proving his ability for self-restraint from an unexpected angle and showing him listening to counsel to boot; he was also apparently willing to eat while actually ill.[99] Jenni Kuuliala has observed that the treatments Charles sought for the lesions caused by the hairshirt demonstrated his "need to balance his saintly corporality with his official duties," just as in other aspects of his spiritual pursuits.[100] Jeanne's intimate access to Charles through their marital relations made her a particularly effective moderating influence. The duke reportedly removed his hairshirt and knotted cords on the nights he slept with his wife and consented to lie on a softer bed with her, literally setting aside his test of endurance to fulfill his carnal and procreative obligations to her and to the ducal line.[101] Michel Barbelot specified that Charles observed additional fasts when he was away from the duchess, implying that her presence encouraged a closer adherence to ordinary behaviour.[102] As the potential distance increased between Charles's two lives, Jeanne's disruption of his pious extremes helped these facets coexist.

On the other hand, the physical responsibilities of lordship were not necessarily so easily reconciled with extreme self-denial, as Charles allegedly

97 D10.9, 17.8.

98 Cf. Thibodeaux, *Manly Priest*, 19.

99 D12.8, 36.7, 46.8, 55.4.

100 D23.11, 47.7; Kuuliala, *Saints, Infirmity, and Community*, 167.

101 D9.12, 10.9, 24.4, 27.7, 31.10, 32.5, 47.7.

102 D47.6.

risked weakening himself even to the point of jeopardizing his martial abilities. One of Charles's chamberlains believed Charles's weakness astonished his physicians, who did not know its source, but this impression was either ignorance or exaggeration.[103] Several of Charles's companions recalled *maître* Georges de Lesnen, in particular, reprimanding the duke for diminishing his bodily strength through fasting or "killing himself" through penance.[104] Georges corroborated their claims, and recalled having roped Charles's confessor into his cause.[105] Similarly, Charles's almoner and chaplain recalled that Charles wore out his body by depriving himself of sleep and food, and his snowy pilgrimage required an extended recovery period.[106] Episodes of illness were among the adversities which Charles suffered patiently; somewhat perversely, Charles even pretended illness in order to fast, as his attendants noticed.[107] Spiritual resilience here came at the cost of bodily fitness.

Evaluated from an aristocratic perspective, these extremes of physical suffering were potentially problematic on several levels. In practical terms, being unwell might inhibit Charles's ability to lead and/or fight himself. On a more conceptual level health could be equated with "the ability to fulfil one's social role," such that neglecting the one meant neglecting the other.[108] More concretely, ill health undermined a knight's control over his body, threatening his masculinity.[109] In this text, infirmity was more usually associated with the poor unfortunates (and even *impotentes*, powerless people) to whom Charles repeatedly tended.[110] Weakness was not a condition that befitted his high status.

However, this simple dichotomy was complicated by the fact that Charles's devotional trials were closely bound up with his ducal career. Many witnesses stressed how his austerities developed in step with the significant milestones of his life. Some who had known Charles in his youth reported that his fasting and penance increased as he aged, suggesting these practices were part of his becoming a man.[111] One of the rare servants

103 D24.3.

104 D12.8, 15.10.

105 D9.6.

106 D35.8; D10.3, 28.9, 38.13, 45.8.

107 D19.3, 26.3, 27.8, 51.7; D10.4, 47.6.

108 Kuuliala, *Saints, Infirmity, and Community*, 167.

109 Bateman, "Knight Fever," 40; Phillips, "Crusader Masculinities."

110 D30.4, 31.5.

111 D1.4, 2.8.

to come with him from Blois to Brittany, Poulet de La Vicogne, believed Charles started wearing the hairshirt after marrying Jeanne, and sleeping without a mattress after his capture at La Roche-Derrien.[112] As Charles became first a husband and then forcibly separated from the marriage bed, he began to express his rigours in new ways. Poulet noted that he observed these habits while Charles was count of Penthièvre and duke of Brittany, the double title emphasizing the growing authority Charles exercised via his wife.[113] Timelines of Charles's asceticism differed; another early companion recalled Poulet telling him Charles slept without a mattress while still under his father's roof.[114] Still, there was largely consensus that he increased his ordeals during his imprisonment, and that he wore his hairshirt to the battle of Auray.[115] Charles's asceticism became a manifestation of his authority and the war he fought.

Linking significant defeats to Charles's asceticism and its physical consequences may have helped some witnesses "make sense of a military fiasco," and the association certainly bolstered the overall martyrdom narrative.[116] More positively, though, fusing martial and spiritual trials underscored Charles's exceptional masculinity. Historians such as Steven Bruso and Katherine Allen Smith have examined the importance of sheer physical hardness to conceptions of knightly masculinity.[117] Hard bodies reflected not only the knight's need to develop enough strength and fitness to wear armour and wield weapons effectively, but also their ability to maintain stamina and withstand pain through sheer toughness. Conversely, medieval moralists habitually voiced concerns over the growing softness and effeminacy of contemporary knights.[118] In Charles's case, his devotional practices were a chance to showcase his hardness. Charles removed the mattress from his bed to make it harder (*durius*), with the implication that the person sleeping upon it must be hard also.[119] That he pursued these sleeping arrangements and other austerities even while on campaign showed their compatibility

112 D52.9.

113 Cf. D41.3.

114 D5.8.

115 E.g., D34.9, 35.8, 41.9.

116 Kuuliala, *Saints, Infirmity, and Community*, 190.

117 Bruso, "Bodies Hardened for War"; Smith, "Saints in Shining Armor," 593; cf. Downes et al., "Introduction—War as Emotion," 10.

118 Dressler, "Steel Corpse," 88; Parsons, "'Loved Him—Hated Her,'" 289–90.

119 D46.7, 51.9, 55.8.

with, and even reinforcement of, the knightly lifestyle.[120] One squire noticed the bare bed when he went to report the progress of the (successful) siege of Carhaix to the duke in 1342.[121] Here, Charles literally commanded from atop a testament of his hardness.[122]

To evaluate such physical masculinity, the usual metric was other men. Charles was even able to outcompete his fellow knights by pitting his ascetic rigours against their more ordinary performance of knighthood. An attendant of Jeanne's uncle Hervé, Hamon de Languéouez, recalled when Hervé once shared Charles's bed for the night.[123] Bed-sharing was part of the culture of martial companionship surrounding the medieval male nobility, reinforcing political and military bonds.[124] Despite usually allowing a relaxation of masculine competition, however, this encounter showed that Charles possessed greater fortitude than his kinsman. Hamon was given a heads-up by Charles's regular servants that once Hervé was asleep, Charles would abandon the luxurious bed for a small, low cot without straw or feather mattress. Come morning, Hamon was treated to a guided tour of Charles's various instruments of penance. Juxtaposing the two men distinguished Charles from one of the greatest noblemen of his duchy. Moreover, Hervé's younger brother Érard recalled that Hervé himself had given Charles a hairshirt early in their acquaintance, when they were together in the royal army.[125] Not only was this gift considered appropriate between knights out in the field, it enabled Charles to push the limits of his toughness further.[126]

Because Charles's baseline bodily existence was more challenging than that of ordinary knights, the fact that he could still fight meant going above and beyond the masculine norm. Facing physical damage and carrying on were essential proofs of knightly manhood.[127] His remark to an attendant squire, astonished at his ability to tolerate his hairshirt, that it was no different from wearing fine undergarments, showed how far he had hardened

---

120 E.g., D12.7, 19.10, 21.9, 24.4, 28.8.

121 D40.6.

122 On the significance of beds to rulership in late medieval France, see Brown and Famiglietti, *Lit de justice*, esp. 21–22.

123 D11.3.

124 Storey, "Questioning Terminologies," 35–36, 40.

125 D57.6.

126 Cf. Constable, "Attitudes Toward Self-Inflicted Suffering," 19.

127 Casey, "Feeling It Like a Man," 243.

himself by the end of his life.[128] Crucially, this exceptional toughness held true even in defeat. By increasing his austerities after his capture at La Roche-Derrien, Charles showed his capacity to withstand yet greater hardship. His physician Georges de Lesnen clarified how Charles's renunciation of mattresses had come about:

> In being captured he was injured with seventeen wounds, which this witness saw. He saw also that after [Charles] was captured, a certain English knight called Lord Thomas Dagworth, in the place where Lord Charles was lying naked on a certain bed with a stuffed feather mattress, angrily had the mattress pulled out from under him. And so the said Lord Charles remained lying upon straw with only a linen sheet over it, for which he gave thanks to God, saying that he wished and desired to be in that state, and that he would never again lie upon a feather mattress.[129]

Charles's battle wounds, successfully borne, led seamlessly into another fight with the enemy, which the duke was likewise able to tough out: by meeting Thomas's challenge he set himself an even higher standard going forward. The interchange of clerical and knightly rigours then continued during his captivity. Since Charles did not ride during this period, he added the same coarse fabric of his hairshirt to his thighs.[130] This alteration attested both the limits he normally kept to in the pursuit of his duty and his refusal to go easy on himself when barred from that pursuit.[131] Set apart from the war, he inflicted wounds upon himself through self-flagellation.[132] Charles remained hard by fighting both earthly and spiritual battles.

His final battle of Auray was the ultimate example of this fortitude. Charles allegedly suffered from an unspecified illness in the weeks leading up to the fight, during which he continued to sleep without a mattress.[133] The servants of his bedchamber reproved Charles for seeking a fight under such conditions, but they received a stern rebuff: "I go to defend my people; only let it please God that the conflict should be between me and my adversary alone, without anyone else having to die because of it."[134] This was a fine line to walk—going to battle unwell could be seen as foolhardy rather

128 D21.9.

129 D9.3.

130 D10.9, 12.7.

131 For Charles's forced inactivity during his captivity, see D9.4.

132 D9.13, 10.9.

133 D19.3, 26.3, 27.8.

134 D27.8.

than noble, but allowing oneself to be put out of action was unmanly.[135] Fortunately, playing different masculine norms against each other had served Charles well before, as when he pointed out that breaking his fast to build up his strength would only encourage the demands of his flesh, and so threaten his self-control.[136] Thus, even in his weakness, Charles was outstanding: he continued to fulfill his lordly obligations both by fighting and by defending his people, and even aspired to be the sole combatant on the field, testing his chivalric mettle.

Charles's death consolidated the blend of sacred and secular masculinity. If at Quimper the duke had removed his armour to invoke God's blessing, here his armour encased his piety as represented by his hairshirt. Hairshirts were Charles's most important open secret: he purportedly favoured white ones because black was too visible, yet they were repeatedly discovered during his close interactions with his men-at-arms.[137] One squire felt the hairshirt when massaging Charles's shoulder after a riding mishap.[138] A knight who fought at Auray had often tried to spot the hairshirt without success, as it was too well covered by the duke's other clothes, though another nobleman caught a glimpse while helping Charles arm himself for the fight.[139] Featuring the hairshirt in these martial contexts made it part of the duke's regular battle equipment. The English later discovered his hairshirt when they "disarmed and despoiled" Charles's corpse.[140] It was customary to take the arms and other valuables of those defeated or killed in battle, and the hairshirt now numbered among these prizes. Several witnesses agreed the English recognized its value and divided the hairshirt into pieces to keep, although a Dominican friar insisted instead that they had simply thrown it aside, so he himself had taken it away and preserved it out of devotion to Charles.[141] Even if it was not immediately seen as a relic (or, we might suspect, a souvenir of victory), the English and Montfortist Bretons apparently discussed the find, suggesting they attached at least some significance to it.[142] The association of temporal and spiri-

135 Bateman, "Knight Fever," 47; Casey, "Feeling It Like a Man," 243.

136 D10.4.

137 D23.11.

138 D21.9.

139 D13.4, 56.6.

140 D9.15, 16.7, 30.8, 40.6, 47.7.

141 D13.4, 40.6, 47.7, 56.6; D30.8.

142 D13.4, 20.4, 32.5, 40.6, 56.6.

tual armour had been exemplified during the high medieval period by the *loricatus*, ascetics who wore armour as part of their penitential routine (often, indeed, along with a hairshirt).[143] This model suited warriors who had become holy men, and while such saints had declined in popularity by the fourteenth century, Charles made something of a *loricatus* in reverse, pushed into the secular life but adopting the trappings of his other path to harness the masculine authority of both roles.

The close association between Charles's piety, his gender, and his leadership in this testimony had ramifications for Jeanne's own reputation. If she was often used passively to contextualize what Charles did and did not do, she could also interact more dynamically with the markers of his exceptionality. For instance, Auray was not the final appearance of the famed hairshirt. In three reports of the aftermath of Charles's death, Jeanne was at Nantes, one of Brittany's two capital cities, and needed funds to leave for Angers, outside the duchy.[144] She ordered a locked chest thought to hold some of Charles's treasury to be opened, but the search found no money, only a box with three hairshirts inside. The symbolic interpretation was obvious: where an ordinary prince, here exemplified by Jeanne, might keep worldly wealth, Charles instead kept items of spiritual value.[145] While this comparison enhanced Charles's saintly credentials, it also set expectations for Jeanne's leadership. Her agency in this scene, one of the few places where her motivations came into view, allowed her to exercise her own set of seigneurial priorities, focusing on practicalities over principles. She thus shared in the ducal authority but visibly took command as an independent actor.

Recognizing Jeanne's agency also meant complicating her default significance through the dynamics of partnership. Whereas many of Charles's valets had him abandon his unpadded bed to visit his wife, one instead reported that their shared bed was divided: "namely, the part in which his wife lay had a feather mattress and pillow, and the part in which the said Lord Charles lay had straw and a mat."[146] Charles and Jeanne were here physically placed on opposite sides, with her sleeping as appropriate for both a duchess and a woman, and him eschewing such worldly luxuries and soft-

143 Smith, "Saints in Shining Armor."

144 D33.7, 35.8, 50.9.

145 We do know that Jeanne kept a piece of one of Charles's hairshirts until her death: La Borderie, ed., *Inventaire*, 6.

146 D10.9.

ness. This contrast gave them each a clear place in the social order. Moreover, while previous studies of this canonization have focused on Jeanne's exclusion from Charles's religious practices, she could instead contribute to them.[147] Two other manservants claimed that the bed was made up the same way for the pair of them as when Charles was alone.[148] Jeanne herself even allegedly took an active hand in promoting this shared arrangement. Repeatedly confronted with the divided bed, "she did not long permit this when she saw it; instead, the said lady duchess lay down with him upon the mat or pad or other prickly mattress." This interpretation, too, reinforced Charles's leadership as he set an example for his spouse to follow, making the household a microcosm of the principality. It was also more fitting for a saint's wife to be worthy of him.[149] But by altering Charles's arrangements, Jeanne participated in the "hardening" of the bed, which lost its connotations of marriage and became more like the rough quarters associated with Charles's military campaigns. Likewise, Jeanne's ability to compete with her husband (a task at which knights had failed) made her his double more than his opposite. And the episode again attested the duchess's authority, as she overruled Charles's attempt to keep her separate.

Indeed, Jeanne's effectiveness as a point of either comparison or contrast with Charles made sense largely because she and he were understood as part of a whole, a married couple and ruling partnership. The lens of shared power underpinned the Franciscan Jean Lay's emphasis on how many sermons Charles listened to when he was in Jeanne's company.[150] He also recalled that Charles fed the poor when he and the duchess happened to be in the same place.[151] To some extent this view was simply practical: Jean was Jeanne's own priest, so he necessarily observed Charles only when the couple was together. Nevertheless, the duchess's presence was not merely incidental to these pious acts. Jean reported that Charles fed an increased number of paupers after he had inherited the duchy, again reflecting the stages of his authority by marriage. Jean also noted that he had been called upon to select them specifically in his role as Jeanne's almoner, implicating her in this process alongside her husband. Similarly, while most witnesses attributed the patronage of churches and institutions to Charles alone, two

147 Esp. Vauchez, *Sainteté*, 422.

148 D27.7.

149 Weissenberg, "Sacrament of Marriage," 463.

150 D34.2.

151 D34.5.

priests recalled having seen letters of foundation for certain projects drawn up on the joint orders of the ducal couple.[152] Jeanne's involvement would have been normal for a noblewoman, but bringing her up here was a deliberate decision that made shared authority relevant to Charles's sanctity. When the ducal pair acted in concert, it reinforced the validity of Charles's behaviour, whether measured against lay or clerical norms; when they diverged, it underscored his exceptionality. In either case, Jeanne's position as duchess was integral to the assessment.

The dynamics of gender and partnership within the canonization process open alternate perspectives on the socio-cultural construction of political reputations. As I showed in the previous section, breaking lordship down into its component parts helped witnesses assert Charles's continuous authority across a challenging period. Distinguishing between Charles's sacred and secular callings likewise offered a strategy for reinterpreting the tensions of the past, but for many witnesses it was just as important that these roles could complement each other. Proving Charles's manliness through spiritual discipline allowed him to satisfy the expectations of knightly competition and offset the need to distance Charles from a conventionally masculine performance of lordship in more martial contexts. By masculinizing or feminizing his authority by turns, the witnesses associated Charles with the full range of gendered expectations of rulership without recourse to narratively inappropriate displays of prowess.

But as Mark Ormrod has shown, the shared participation of both kings and queens in the gendered responsibilities of monarchy could disturb contemporary hierarchies of power. He argues that in late medieval England, there was thus a tendency to masculinize royal holiness, where the sanctity of kings was used in part to reassert their authority independent of their wives.[153] In Charles's canonization we find quite a different approach, or rather approaches. Most witnesses focused on Charles alone, as appropriate for the occasion. This exclusivity could have helped draw attention to his self-sufficient, manly authority, but the specific political context demanded a more complicated gendering of his role. Meanwhile, other witnesses included Jeanne, often in a similar function to the "barons and others of his duchy" surrounding Charles—of whom she was, in effect, the most preeminent. Jeanne's gender and authority, however, made her stand out from the noble crowd. On one hand, she represented a feminized presence that more

152 D23.9, 26.9.

153 Ormrod, "Monarchy, Martyrdom, and Masculinity," 186–87.

clearly defined Charles's self-control, and certainly did not defy any binary norms. On the other hand, her own lordship offered an immediate metric for his, and was accordingly gendered more malleably. She could participate alongside Charles in several of his activities, rather than competing with him like a knight or taking over the pious duties of rulers often left to women. Their mirroring relied on and reinforced the fundamental unity of the spousal couple as rulers, even as each retained their own agency. A flexible view of such gendered partnerships ultimately contributed to the stability of lordship.

Conclusions

Charles's and Jeanne's reputations in the canonization process give a more holistic appreciation of the standards by which an elite, largely male audience evaluated princely leadership. Canonization was a politically effective strategy in the late Middle Ages precisely because it did not respond to the needs of the Church alone, but appealed to the kinds of people footing the bill.[154] Yet as with the identification of sainthood itself, there was no definitive checklist for an "orthodox" lord. While moral authorities offered models for their aristocratic readers throughout the medieval period, good reputation here did not rely on conformity to a single archetype.[155] Instead, from the perspective of politics as constant crisis, the best lord was the one that fit the occasion. Moreover, efforts to normalize Charles's tenure as duke by elevating him above the civil war on the one hand, and by anchoring his conduct in noble values on the other, relied on his associations with others. As his wife and as a parallel repository for ducal authority, Jeanne provided a ready benchmark and/or counterpoint. In this interpretation, legitimacy became a collaborative project.

Did these reputations reach beyond the immediate context? Theoretically, these testimonies were supposed to represent the wider community. Every *vita* witness confirmed that what they had reported was also "commonly said, held, and told" in their area. This *fama* was both part of the justification for sanctity, and the means by which news of it spread.[156] We can see this process in action in the presentation of evidence by local notables in front of a large crowd at the town of Lamballe in Penthièvre. Similarly,

154 Smoller, "Northern and Southern Sanctity," 290, 308.

155 Crouch, *Chivalric Turn*; Wittig, *Learning to Be Noble*, esp. chap. 4.

156 Krötzl, "*Fama sanctitatis*."

the inhabitants of Guingamp wrote a collective letter to the papal commission that both stressed Charles's particular relationship with their town and confirmed his pious generosity, his protection of the weak, and his ascetic hardships.[157] The military companies of Breton nobles and mercenaries who travelled far afield, as well as the Franciscan order, also contributed to the publicity.[158]

At the same time, the files produced by the papal examiners were not a matter of public record, and did not circulate in written form among wider audiences. As Jeanne's and Charles's reputations developed in other narrative formats, then, there was no direct link back to the canonization materials. However, some of the details captured in the chronicle tradition attest their ongoing dissemination via word-of-mouth across elite networks. Moreover, if I have focused here only on certain issues with which the witnesses grappled (especially ones neglected by earlier studies of this testimony), these themes continued to play out in new contexts. The relative responsibility for warfare, the gendered and un-gendered performance of good lordship, and the two-way influence of partnered reputations were far from settled, and the same events could be reinterpreted no less authentically in a new light.

157 Both reports were transcribed as part of the canonization dossier as R19 and R16, respectively.

158 E.g., Héry et al., eds., *Procès de canonisation*, 156n279; D32.10; Cassard, "*Gestes des Bretons*," 105; Vauchez, "Canonisation et politique."

Chapter 2

CHIVALRIC CONNECTIONS

ON THE HEELS of Charles's near-canonization in 1376, the political landscape evolved rapidly. King Charles V confiscated the duchy in 1379, dispossessing both Jeanne de Penthièvre and Jean IV despite the legal cases made in their favour. A Breton rebellion ensued, in which Jeanne remained ostensibly neutral while networking with those who opposed the French king. Duke Jean's recall from exile and effective military resistance led to the second treaty of Guérande in 1381, reestablishing the terms agreed at the end of the war of succession. Jeanne herself died in 1384, but the long-delayed release of her eldest son Jean from English captivity in 1387 further provoked sporadic armed conflict that would carry over into the next generation.[1] Meanwhile, from 1370 to 1407 the position of royal military commander (*connétable*) was held by powerful Breton noblemen who opposed the Montfortists, first Bertrand du Guesclin, who had fought for Jeanne and Charles during the civil war, then Olivier de Clisson, father-in-law to Jean de Penthièvre. However, King Charles VI's mental instability precluded further French military intervention in the duchy after 1392, and his daughter Jeanne married the future Duke Jean V in 1396. Against this backdrop of shifting tensions and affiliations, new historical accounts developed to frame the Breton civil war and its participants in a martial light.

By examining Jeanne's and Charles's posthumous reputations in the framework of what may be termed "chivalric" chronicles, preoccupied with feats of arms and aristocratic values, a very different picture emerges from that in the canonization proceedings. In the histories written by Froissart and Cuvelier, the war took centre stage rather than being excused. Its violence brought suffering to the duchy and its inhabitants, but also, indeed primarily, enabled extraordinary deeds. The expected standards of behaviour were no longer couched in clerical terms, but engaged more directly with the performance of knighthood. And whereas Jeanne's characterization had previously depended on the parameters established for Charles, the widening of the narrative scope now made the influence more independently bi-directional. Nevertheless, the audience for these works was

1 Lémeillat, "Jean et Olivier de Bretagne," 71–74, 77–79.

socially similar to the witnesses who testified at Angers, and the events of the early 1370s were still relatively fresh within elite circles. This overlapping outlook meant that some of the same stories, themes, and interpretations from the first phase of their reputational development found new life in the chronicle tradition.

This second phase participated in a booming period of chivalric writing, and in particular of chivalric biographies that advocated their protagonist's virtues to consolidate their knightly legacy.[2] But whereas many of these works were preoccupied with the accomplishments of individual men, the treatment of the Breton civil war allowed the dynamics of the ducal couple to come to the fore. The interplay of Jeanne's and Charles's roles shows how structural mechanisms for acquiring and delegating power could rework the usual patterns of military leadership.[3] This two-way exchange further extends our understanding of seigneurial partnerships, where a husband's ability to act (systematically) on behalf of his wife, or a wife (periodically) on behalf of her husband, have been treated largely in isolation rather than as part of a single process, and adds a gendered dimension to our assessment of how elite networks played into civil wars.[4] Moreover, as knightly honour was keyed to martial masculinity, the extent to which noblewomen were able to reach these standards has been much debated, both then and now.[5] The reciprocity between the duke and duchess here suggests that lordly women could be routinely integrated into this normative framework with or without crossing gendered lines, and the success or failure of both men and women according to chivalric standards took on new explanatory weight in divergent assessments of shared power.

Chivalric Reputations

Whereas the canonization proceedings packaged disparate testimony into an ostensibly coherent whole, the chivalric accounts dressed their basic story in layered reinterpretations. The two narratives taking the spotlight in this chapter were originally the work of two contemporary ecclesiastics, Jean Froissart and Cuvelier, probably both of Picard origin (a dialectal region

2 Taylor, *Virtuous Knight*, 1–5.

3 A preliminary version of some of this research appeared in Graham-Goering, "Authority."

4 E.g., Bolton and Meek, *Aspects of Power*, 1; LoPrete, "Women, Gender and Lordship," 1924–26, 1929, 1931.

5 LoPrete, "Gendering Viragos."

in northeastern France). Very little is known about Cuvelier, whose identity can only be deduced from clues in his work. He appears to have been a cleric, probably associated with the French royal court, who died between 1384 and 1389.[6] Froissart's life is much better-documented.[7] He was born around 1337 in the county of Hainault, at the modern-day border of France and Belgium. His first literary patron was Philippa of Hainault, queen of England by her marriage to Edward III, for whom he wrote a now-lost poetic chronicle. After her death in 1369, he returned to his hometown of Valenciennes and pursued several church benefices while building his writing career with the support of various great magnates connected to the courts of both France and England. Of these patrons, the most significant from the point of view of the Breton conflict was Guy de Châtillon (d. 1397), count of Blois and Charles's nephew. Froissart's extensive travels in France, Great Britain, and Italy also put him in contact with many of the other major political players of his day. While the precise date of his death is unknown, he continued to write until after 1404, though his chronicle ends with events in 1400. Both Froissart's chronicle and Cuvelier's poem thus developed in a similar context and from similar perspectives. They were vernacular works written about and for, but not by, the knightly aristocracy following the winding down of the Breton war.

However, each of these works were also much more than a polished interpretation of events by a single person. Froissart's chronicle, for instance, was a medieval bestseller, with over 150 known manuscripts, though its popularity in France increased during the fifteenth century.[8] It is conventionally divided into four parts: Book I (covering roughly the years 1307–1378), Book II (1379–1384), Book III (1386–1391), and Book IV (1392–1400), totalling about 1.5 million words. The "matter of Brittany," as Froissart called it, fell into the first book, which survives in around 60 manuscripts. And because Froissart was reluctant to leave well enough alone, we have seven different versions of Book I, in addition to other variations introduced by the people who copied specific manuscripts. To study how Jeanne's and Charles's reputations developed in his work, we can focus on four variants, known as Amiens (composed between 1384 and 1391),

6 Cuvelier, *Chanson de Bertrand du Guesclin*, ed. Faucon, 3:36–37.

7 Ainsworth, "Froissart, Jean"; Ainsworth, "Jean Froissart: Chronicler, Poet and Writer"; Croenen, "Froissart et ses mécènes."

8 Croenen, "Reception," 410; Tesnière, "Manuscrits copiés par Raoul Tainguy," 302; Courroux, *Écriture de l'histoire*, 368, 936; Guenée, *Du Guesclin et Froissart*, 174–75, 180–83.

B (1391–1399), and Rome (1404 or later), as well as an Abridged version written around the same time as Amiens.[9] The Amiens, Rome, and Abridged versions survive in only a single manuscript each, the first two named for the libraries where these are now kept. Unfortunately, the Rome manuscript is incomplete, so the surviving text of Book I only records events up to 1350. Of these four it was the B text, or large excerpts thereof, that was circulated most widely in the medieval period, so insofar as reputation reflected common opinion, it should be seen as the most representative. However, its narrative decisions can only be understood in comparison with the alternatives Froissart explored elsewhere.

Even figuring out what order these versions were composed in has been challenging for historians. A key sticking point is that Froissart himself based portions of his work on an earlier chronicle written by Jean Le Bel. Le Bel was another Picard churchman, serving as a canon of Liège in what is now Belgium.[10] He wrote a chronicle of Edward III's reign from 1326 to 1361 at the request of Jean, lord of Beaumont, Queen Philippa's uncle, whom Le Bel accompanied to England and Scotland in 1327. This account was relatively little known in its own right, with only one manuscript surviving.[11] Because Froissart sometimes drew heavily and explicitly on Le Bel's chronicle, scholars since the late nineteenth century have often assumed that versions that stuck closer to this source were written earlier, and more independent versions came later. In some parts of the text this was true, but Froissart's representations of the Breton civil war were less strictly linear. Godfried Croenen has identified several considerations that influenced Froissart's decisions, from updating his information, to enhancing dramatic or realistic descriptions, to constructing a coherent narrative—not all necessarily compatible motivations.[12] Moreover, Froissart kept his other versions to hand (including Le Bel) and may even have developed some simultaneously, so he could freely rework the text by innovating in some places or reverting to a trusted textual authority in others. Accord-

9 For this chronology, see Croenen, "Guerre en Normandie," 142. Respectively, these four versions have been edited in Froissart, *Chroniques: Livre I*, ed. Diller (hereafter Amiens); *Chroniques de J. Froissart*, ed. Luce (hereafter FrB); *Œuvres de Froissart*, ed. Kervyn de Lettenhove (hereafter Abridged); Froissart, *Chroniques: Dernière rédaction*, ed. Diller (hereafter Rome).

10 Croenen, "Jean Le Bel."

11 See Le Bel, *Chronique*, for the French text, and Le Bel, *True Chronicles*, for an English translation.

12 Croenen, "Guerre en Normandie," 142.

ingly, each new version was not an "improvement" on the last or working towards a definitive account of the conflict, but used different possibilities to interpret past events.[13]

How we use Froissart as a historical source has changed substantially over time. While he was long regarded as a, or indeed the, authority on the events of the Hundred Years' War, skepticism from the later nineteenth century onwards about his factual reliability has led more recent scholars to emphasize Froissart's value as a reflection of the mindset of his social circle.[14] Book I opened with a clear statement of Froissart's goals in writing the chronicle. He hoped to record the "great deeds of arms" of the wars between France and England, so that they could be widely known and forever recalled as instructive exemplars.[15] This focus on martial feats has earned him the moniker of the "chronicler of chivalry" among some modern historians, not all of whom view it as a good thing.[16] Rather than underestimating conventional portrayals of aristocratic action as "servile," however, we can consider how they constructed reputation in specific ways.[17] First for our purposes, Froissart's focus on feats of arms meant that his narrative of the Breton civil war was structured around certain highlights of the conflict. The opening years of the war were discussed in greatest depth; then Froissart picked up on Charles's capture at La Roche-Derrien in 1347, the Combat of Thirty of 1351, and finally the battle of Auray. Jeanne's and Charles's reputations consolidated around these set-piece encounters, but continued to reflect a range of ideas about lordship, gender, and shared power.

Second, Froissart's aim to commemorate and inform meant he usually selected positive illustrations of aristocratic values and behaviour, though it has been noted that the final, Rome version assumed a bleaker tone.[18] His noble audience wanted to see themselves reflected in these stories, and were even the source for many of them.[19] In his prologue Froissart noted that he had spoken with the "valiant men, knights and squires" who had taken part in these events, supplementing his own eyewitness testimony. For Brittany

13 Palmer, "Book I," 24; cf. Courroux, *Écriture de l'histoire*, 352, 366.

14 Jones, "Breton Civil War."

15 Amiens, 1:1; FrB, 1.2:1; Rome, 35.

16 Coulton, *Chronicler of European Chivalry*.

17 Ainsworth, "Froissardian Perspectives," 62.

18 Froissart, *Chroniques: Dernière rédaction*, ed. Diller, 22.

19 Courroux, *Écriture de l'histoire*, 369.

specifically, Froissart visited the duchy in 1366, and spoke with the former Penthièvre knight Even Charruel in 1373–1374 and possibly with Guillaume de Saint-Mesmin, one of Charles's physicians, in 1388.[20] Through such dialogue Froissart sought a historical truth that lay less in strict facts than in what was plausibly understood to have happened and its significance.[21] In other words, he tried to create a permanent record of good *fama*, though as Froissart's constant rewritings (and other non-authorial additions) show, the process of reputation was not so easily pinned down.

Cuvelier, by comparison, personally wrote only one version of his poetic life and deeds of Bertrand du Guesclin (ca. 1320–1380), constable of France.[22] The scope of this work, finished around 1384, was quite unlike Froissart's chronicle—Cuvelier termed it not a chronicle or history, but a *roman*, or heroic narrative.[23] It focused on a single individual, used the poetic format which was increasingly coming under suspicion for distorting truth in favour of rhyme, was substantially shorter (at 24,346 lines) than Froissart's work, and enjoyed a much more modest, albeit still considerable, manuscript circulation (eight are known to survive).[24] As an example of chivalric biography, it nevertheless belonged to the same world of grand military exploits and idealized aristocratic culture that flourished in the late Middle Ages.[25] These shared interests make it fruitful to compare how Cuvelier's and Froissart's narratives approached the figures of the duke and duchess in the context of the civil war.

Adding a layer of complexity, however, Cuvelier's poem was rewritten in prose not once but twice within five years of its completion. We know nothing of the authors of these texts, but unlike the poem we have a good idea of when and for whom they were written.[26] The first prose version (A) was commissioned in 1387 by Jeannet d'Estouteville, a Norman at the French

---

20 Jones, "Ancenis," 93; FrB, 4:115; Jones, "Breton Civil War," 73–74; Froissart, *Œuvres*, ed. Kervyn de Lettenhove, 1.1:318.

21 Ainsworth, "Contemporary and 'Eyewitness' History," 270; Froissart, *Chroniques*, ed. Luce, 1.1:cviii–ix; Courroux, *Écriture de l'histoire*, 819–57.

22 See Cuvelier, *Chanson de Bertrand du Guesclin*, ed. Faucon, vol. 1 (hereafter Chanson), for the French text; and Cuvelier, *Song of Bertrand du Guesclin*, for an English translation.

23 Cuvelier, *Chanson de Bertrand du Guesclin*, ed. Faucon, 3:39.

24 Ainsworth, *Jean Froissart and the Fabric of History*, 36–46; Cuvelier, *Chanson de Bertrand du Guesclin*, ed. Faucon, 3:311–12, 329.

25 Taylor, *Virtuous Knight*, 1–5.

26 Vermijn, "'De quoy juqu'a mille ans bien parlé en sera,'" appendix 1.

royal court with personal and familial connections to the constable.[27] It condensed the original length by about a third, but remained largely faithful to the overall narrative. The second prose version (B) was written around 1389 at the command of Jeanne and Charles's daughter Marie de Bretagne, duchess of Anjou.[28] It was much freer than the A version in terms of both style, which became more like that of a chronicle than an epic, and content, particularly to develop the role played by Marie and her family. The A version survives in eight manuscripts, the B version in twelve (plus four of an abridged text), suggesting a successful uptake in each case, and both would be set into printed editions in the fifteenth and sixteenth centuries. The poem and both prose texts circulated at the royal court and among the northern French nobility, while the A version also enjoyed a certain popularity in Burgundian circles. Yvonne Vermijn suggests that the coexistence of all three versions meant they inspired variations in each other in subsequent copies.[29] While Cuvelier was not involved in revising his work as Froissart had been, the end result was similarly diffuse, evolving in several directions without establishing a definitive form.

The chronological overlap in the composition of Froissart's *Chroniques* and Cuvelier's *Chanson* and their appeal to similar audiences gives focus to the political positioning of these works and how it shaped their framing of the Breton conflict on multiple levels. Froissart claimed, famously, to be impartial in the contest between the kings of France and England. His exemplary knights represented both sides (an even-handed praise that could, to partisans, nevertheless appear hostile) and he took no position on the core issues that set the kings at odds. However, equitable reporting could still capture different strands of public opinion. Froissart's characters held views on the legitimacy of the claimants in Brittany, and his own understanding of the war evolved over time. More subtly, a chronicler's neutrality might be no better than that of their sources. Jean Le Bel, sympathetic to the English as he was, was still susceptible to Valois spin, seen in an erroneous Montfort genealogy that persisted throughout Froissart's rewritings.[30] Certain manuscript copyists, in turn, attempted to correct such libel.[31] This reiterative process shows how such chronicles lived within a wider political

27 Ménard, ed., *Histoire de messire Bertrand du Guesclin* (hereafter PGA).

28 Buchon, ed., "Chronique anonyme" (hereafter PGB).

29 Vermijn, "Chacun son Guesclin," 31–36.

30 Chareyron, *Jean Le Bel*, 209.

31 Mazzei, "Two Claimants," 154n10.

discourse, and the reputations in their works were unavoidably shaped by these currents.

Cuvelier's emphatic pro-French stance contrasts with Froissart's more international perspective, as does the place of the civil war in his work. Charles, and especially Jeanne, were only supporting characters in Cuvelier's story of the constable, so their reputations were somewhat incidental to the work's panegyric function. Insofar as Bertrand fought on their side, Cuvelier was sympathetic to their cause. At the same time, he was active in the French court when Charles V fell out with Jeanne de Penthièvre, who contested the king's attempted annexation of the duchy in 1379–1380. On top of this conflict of interest regarding Breton affairs, Cuvelier's active misogyny coloured his approach to gender dynamics differently from Froissart's.[32] Conversely, his adaptors and later copyists did not necessarily share these views and updated the text accordingly. Some later copies of the poem and of the Prose Guesclin A were more critical of Charles V or modified various characters' roles to reflect contemporary political fortunes.[33] Marie de Bretagne's commission predictably expanded on certain episodes of the war and enhanced the portrayal of its protagonists where needed. Again, the ongoing political value of these works meant an author's initial interpretation was not the end of the story.

Finally, chronicles responded not only to external political contexts, but also to each other. I have already discussed how different versions of Le Bel/ Froissart and Cuvelier fed into their own retellings, but the same happened between formerly separate histories. For example, Froissart's A version (ca. 1381) survives only for the beginning and end of the text (which do not concern the Breton war); instead, it was combined with large excerpts of the B version and the unrelated *Grandes chroniques de France* to create a hybrid chronicle that circulated widely under Froissart's attribution.[34] These accounts in turn became the source of rumours and reputations. We can only directly trace their impact on written historiography, but the audiences who read these works or heard them read aloud would have made them part

32 Cuvelier, *Chanson de Bertrand du Guesclin*, ed. Faucon, 3:117–20.

33 Vermijn, "Chacun son Guesclin," 33–34, 42–43.

34 Croenen, "Guerre en Normandie," 118. The *Grandes chroniques* were the official and highly influential history of the French kings, composed at the royal abbey of Saint Denis, then at court, from the thirteenth to fifteenth centuries. The excerpts covered the years 1350–1356 in most of the Froissart manuscripts, although in four copies (MSS A34–37 in Froissart, *Chroniques*, ed. Luce, 1.1:xxxv) the opening years of the Breton war up to Charles's capture are a paraphrase of the *Grandes chroniques*.

of their political dialogues.[35] Both individually and in combination, then, the chivalric narratives of the war of succession fed from and into the cyclical process of creating *fama*.

Legitimizing Status, Gender, and Relationships

If the canonization inquiry stressed that Charles was not born to be duke, the inheritance of lordly status was a defining feature of Jeanne's and Charles's roles in both Froissart and the Guesclin tradition. This framing makes sense when talking about a war of succession, but it also reflected the aristocratic preoccupation with titles and ancestry.[36] For them, leadership was not just about what you *did*; it was part of who you *were*. Jeanne's position as the natural heir of the late Duke Jean III let her automatically claim the loyalty of the Breton nobility. Charles, meanwhile, was a representative of the extended French royal family, granting him both rank and access to a network of friendship and obligation. These distinct types of authority became complementary in marriage, with Jeanne's claim to the duchy reinforced by Charles's friends in high places. Into this mix came a third source of legitimacy, the oaths of fidelity sworn between lords, which helped Charles in particular establish himself as duke. Authority played out across these relationships as both direct command and indirect delegation, complicating the impact of status and gendered roles on princely legitimacy.

The passage of Froissart that best illustrates the fluid outcomes of this framework appears during Jean de Montfort's initial bid to conquer the major Breton towns. His first stop in the chronicle was the fortress of Brest on the western tip of the peninsula, where its captain Garnier de Clisson defied him. Garnier's reasoning, however, differed from version to version.[37] Proceeding chronologically, in Amiens he would not obey Jean because "there was one nearer to the inheritance than was he." In the Abridgement, it was because Garnier held Brest for the heiress, wife of Charles de Blois, to whom he himself was related. The B version claimed Garnier would not accept Jean as lord without clear proof "of the lord to whom it should belong by right." Finally, in the Rome text, Garnier objected first that the Breton barons and the French king must recognize the new duke, then bluntly declared

35 Cuvelier, *Chanson de Bertrand du Guesclin*, ed. Faucon, 3:288–89; Contamine, "En marge."

36 Taylor, *Chivalry and the Ideals of Knighthood*, 55.

37 Amiens, 2:102; Abridged, 107; FrB, 2:91; Rome, 468–69.

that the duchy belonged to Charles by reason of his wife as a daughter of the ducal line. While all four scenes emphasized the orderly structures underpinning legitimate authority, the potential claimant could be either member of the ducal couple, explicitly named or left ambivalent. Consistent factors of status, gender, and relationships could generate inconsistent interpretations of joint lordship.

To unpick these dynamics, I will show how Jeanne and Charles were each situated at a different node of their power networks before turning to how they interacted. For both Froissart and Cuvelier, relationships were key to establishing the respective status of the would-be duke and duchess. All of Froissart's retellings of the Breton war, as well as Le Bel's earlier account, explained that Jean III's heir was the daughter of his younger brother. Jean had married her to Charles de Blois, nephew of the king of France, although he worried that the count of Montfort would attempt to disinherit her.[38] Cuvelier's four-line summary of the war's premise likewise foregrounded Jeanne's inheritance, her marital status, and the Montfortist threat. He explained that there were two heirs claiming to be the late duke's nearest relation: a lady, wife of Charles de Blois, who pursued her rights, and the count of Montfort who wished to take precedence.[39] The Prose Guesclin B further developed the legal logic of the succession, which suggests that the anonymous author had, via their patron, better access to the actual terms of this suit, but otherwise followed the familiar pattern.[40] Putting Jeanne and her lineage first was a deliberate decision. Froissart's and Cuvelier's accounts contrasted with, for example, the *Grandes chroniques*, which were written from the French royal perspective and began instead with Charles's family history.[41] Starting with Jeanne established her claim as the source of authority within Brittany, while Charles provided a link to the higher, external power on which the duchy depended.

Jeanne's and Charles's respective positions shaped in turn the depiction of their leadership, because their status determined how others might follow them and serve their interests. Froissart at times suggested that Jeanne automatically commanded the loyalty of the Breton military captains. In addition to Garnier de Clisson above, the captain of Rennes Henri

38 Amiens, 2:97–98; FrB, 2:87–88; Rome, 462–63; Le Bel, *Chronique*, 1:247–48. For a schematic breakdown of these passages, see Graham-Goering, "Authority," table 1.

39 Chanson, ll. 843–46; cf. PGA, 17.

40 PGB, 4; Graham-Goering et al., *Aux origines de la guerre*, doc. II.

41 Viard, ed., *Grandes chroniques*, 9:218.

d'Espinefort in the Amiens text refused to give up his "rightful lady" and had always considered her the heiress, a view allegedly shared by a thousand other knights and squires. The town's elite agreed that they would never "commit fraud or fail in their loyalty towards their rightful and natural lady."[42] This phrasing emphasized leadership as a structural effect. The adjective *droit(e)*, translated here as "rightful," had several interlocking connotations: legitimate legal and moral entitlement; appropriateness according to reason, truth, and order; and directness or immediacy. Similarly, the concept of a "natural" lord invoked ideas of birthright (and even birthplace), inherent nobility, legitimate rule, and conformity to natural law and order.[43] Casting the duchess's authority in these terms mapped out how it should have worked, a pre-ordained course subverted by Jean de Montfort's intervention (not unlike imagining Charles's uncontested rule in the canonization). Ordinarily, Jeanne could expect loyalty because of who she was.

Charles's position as nephew of the king of France, meanwhile, worked a bit differently. His high birth made him unquestionably a great nobleman, and both chronicle traditions stressed the eminence of his blood and lineage.[44] When it came to converting this personal status into the capacity to command, however, Charles (or the king on his behalf) had to ask for help. Charles could usually rely on kinship bonds to recruit French lords to his cause. Froissart's Rome version was particularly explicit about these family ties, repeatedly referring to major players as Charles's uncle, brother, or cousin.[45] Charles could not demand assistance from these magnates as he was not their lord, but they were generally willing to enter his service upon request, or at least to act as his allies.[46] Of course, the efficacy of these connections relied on affinity, as seen in the contrast between the beginning and end of the war. Froissart emphasized King Philippe VI's closeness to his nephew when explaining his grant of the duchy to Charles and initial assembly of an army in 1341.[47] However, the sense of obligation became more tenuous over generations: by 1364, Philippe's grandson Charles V gave Duke Charles military support more on the basis of the promises made by his pre-

42 Amiens, 2:107, 110–11, 114–15.

43 Krynen, "Naturel," esp. 184; Levasseur, "Dénoncer la tyrannie"; Scordia, "*Il n'est pas sire de son pays*"; Roux, *Dialogues de Salmon*, 22.

44 E.g., Abridged, 105; Rome, 474; Chanson, ll. 3074, 6312; PGA, 36.

45 Rome, e.g., 490, 499, 568, 580; cf. Amiens, 2:143.

46 E.g., Rome, 490; FrB, 2:158; Chanson, l. 2499.

47 Amiens, 2:142; Abridged, 113; FrB, 2:104, 106–7, 116; Rome, 490.

decessors than on his own account.[48] Nevertheless, he lamented the death of his cousin shortly thereafter—and with this kinship connection broken, French aid to the duchy ceased.[49] Through Charles, a conflict between two branches of the Breton ducal family became the project of the French royal family, of which Charles effectively acted as the local representative.

Cuvelier neatly outlined these conceptual counterparts when the duke of Lancaster asked Bertrand du Guesclin to identify his lord. Bertrand replied that it was "Duke Charles de Blois, who was born of the royals, and milady his wife of great excellence, who ought to hold the inheritance of Brittany."[50] Likewise in Froissart's Amiens text, when the duke of Normandy left Brittany after the opening campaign, he had the Breton barons swear to stay loyal to "milord Charles *his* cousin, and his wife, *their* lady."[51] But because both components, inheritance and networks, were necessary for the ducal couple, it was easy for their roles to intertwine. Katrin Sjursen has argued that medieval aristocratic marriages helped establish what she calls a "lordship unit," where both spouses participated in seigneurial authority regardless of their independent relationship to the source of power and, to some extent, regardless of their gender.[52] In Froissart, Charles displayed this parity by commissioning armorial banners befitting "a lord and a lady."[53] Correspondingly, their supporters and allies were motivated to act on behalf of them both together. In the Abridgment, the departing French lords formally took their leave of both Charles and his wife the duchess.[54] Earlier, the captain Olivier de Clisson at La Roche-Periou had sworn that "never would he obey [Jean de Montfort] and would hold no other lord heir of Brittany save for milord Charles de Blois and milady his wife."[55] Meanwhile, Jean de Montfort worried that the French would intervene to "claim the inheritance in the name of milord Charles de Blois and of his wife who called herself

48 Amiens, 3:330; Abridged, 408.

49 Amiens, 3:356; FrB, 6:177–78; Abridged, 419; FrB, 6:173; Chanson, ll. 7278–79, 7284; PGA, 151; PGB, 27.

50 Chanson, ll. 1883–85; cf. PGA, 35.

51 Amiens, 2:301 (my emphasis).

52 Sjursen, "War of the Two Jeannes," 39.

53 Rome, 475–76.

54 Abridged, 118.

55 Abridged, 110.

heiress of it."[56] In all these instances, leadership was a joint attribute resulting from the individual authorities of the duke and duchess.

I suggest, however, that rather than implying equivalent access to ducal authority on both sides, such overlap reflected a mutual dependence that engaged, rather than obscured, personal status and gendered roles, neither of which could exist outside a relational context. For instance, marriage put Jeanne at a disadvantage in gendered terms, and her dependency on Charles is shown overwhelmingly by the fact that these accounts referred to her primarily as his wife. Only the Rome manuscript of Froissart's Book I mentioned her given name, and only at her first introduction.[57] But while Jeanne was subordinated to the generic lordship of her husband, this gendered domination did not affect her direct access to the title of duchess.[58] Meanwhile, her status as heiress permitted her to command despite her sex: "natural" lordship overrode the "natural" subordination of women, keeping Jeanne's leadership within the expected order.

Conversely, on gendered grounds we might expect Charles to have control over his wife's duchy as a matter of course. Froissart indicated this simplified process in Book III, where he reminded his audience that by marrying Jeanne, who "came from the direct stock of Brittany and its dukes," Charles could claim the ducal title.[59] However, the implications were not so clear-cut up close.[60] Le Bel, and so Froissart's B text, claimed that Duke Jean promised Charles the duchy in marriage, but this direct authority apparently came from the duke's commitment rather than by default.[61] Moreover, this line was omitted in the other three versions, which instead emphasized that Charles would defend Jeanne's claim as the rightful heir.[62] Charles's authority therefore stemmed from, rather than supplanting, that of his wife. He was called duke *a cause de* or *de par sa femme*—because of or on behalf of his wife—and so became a proxy who exercised what was actually Jeanne's

56 Rome, 482.

57 Rome, 462. It was also the only version to realize that Jeanne inherited the county of Penthièvre from her mother, rather than gaining it at the treaty of Guérande. Jeanne was again named in Book III: Besançon, Bibliothèque municipale, MS 865, fol. 309v.

58 E.g., Amiens, 3:356; FrB, 6:178–79; Rome, 817.

59 Besançon, BM, MS 865, fol. 309.

60 For another case where a husband's authority was not automatically accepted over that of the heiress, see Blincoe, "Geoffrey le Bel of Anjou," esp. 89.

61 Le Bel, *Chronique,* 1:247; FrB, 2:87.

62 Amiens, 2:97; Abridged, 105; Rome, 463, cf. 468–69.

lordship by delegation.[63] Neither Jeanne's leadership nor Charles's could be fully understood without reference to the other, as their identities combined and recombined to produce different configurations of leadership.

A third, external source of legitimacy then inflected this mutual dependence within the couple. Seigneurial authority was founded on the act of homage, a mutual pledge of loyalty and assistance between two people in a hierarchy. Homage was not, in itself, a masculine prerogative, but its basis in military service made it more readily available to men, especially when acting as their wife's representative. For Brittany, the duke owed homage to the king of France, and would receive homage from the Breton barons. The logic of homage was linked to the logic of legal ownership of the duchy. Accordingly, certain French chronicles of this period did portray Charles and Jeanne jointly performing homage to Philippe VI, or even Jeanne on her own, in recognition of her blood claim.[64] For Froissart and the Prose Guesclin B, however, it offered an alternative channel for Charles to access authority in his own right, rather than remaining dependent on Jeanne.[65] The duchy thereby became his own inheritance. Charles in turn raised an army and began to receive homage from the barons and towns of the duchy.[66] These repeated vows of loyalty were intimately linked with the progress of the war, coming after successful sieges and accompanying the installation of new military officers. For Charles, homage implied an active achievement of lordship that became especially important in light of the contested succession as well as the feats of arms prioritized in a chivalric chronicle.

As a result, these accounts frequently portrayed Charles as sole leader rather than part of a pair. Even Bertrand du Guesclin, on other occasions in Cuvelier's work, tended to stress this singular loyalty. When war broke out, he reasoned that Charles showed a greater right to the duchy and swore to aid him, persuading his fellow knights to join him with promises that Charles would make them all rich.[67] Charles's claim and the obedience he commanded were similarly stressed in several versions of Froissart, as when the (possibly fictitious) bishop Guy de Léon defected from the Montfortists

63 Amiens, 3:333; FrB, 2:102, 305 (A version); Rome, 480; Chanson, ll. 893, 2395–97; PGA, 133; PGB, 5.

64 Moranvillé, ed., *Chronographia regum Francorum*, 2:183; Molinier and Molinier, eds., *Chronique normande*, 50.

65 Le Bel, *Chronique*, 1:263; Amiens, 2:142; FrB, 2:106; Rome, 488; PGB, 5.

66 Abridged, 116; Rome, 492.

67 Chanson, ll. 895–97, 902–3, 959–60, 6217–18; cf. 2376–82, 3465, 6317, and PGB, 10.

to join Charles, or again with Bertrand du Guesclin himself.[68] After capturing the castle of Champtoceaux at the start of the war, Jean duke of Normandy handed it over to Charles "as heir and duke of Brittany" or "as his own and his inheritance."[69] Several of the greatest Breton lords left the duchy rather than join Jean de Montfort, but they knew King Philippe would not allow his nephew to be driven out of his inheritance.[70] His use of the ducal arms independently of Jeanne reflected that of Jean de Montfort pursuing his own claim.[71] Indeed, whereas Cuvelier introduced the disputed succession in Jeanne's name, Froissart invoked the "cause and right" which Charles had to the inheritance of Brittany, eclipsing Jeanne.[72]

Having direct authority mattered precisely because of the persistent ambiguity engendered by Jeanne and Charles's mutual dependence. Compare Froissart's Abridgement, where Charles "believed himself to be the rightful heir of Brittany," to the A text, where he "believed himself, by reason of his wife, to be the rightful heir of Brittany."[73] The Amiens manuscript directly juxtaposed Charles, who saw himself as heir on his wife's behalf, with King Philippe, who supported his nephew as heir.[74] In the B version, Charles summoned the nobles who had done him homage to help guard and defend his inheritance against his foes, but in Amiens they had done homage because they considered him duke and lord on behalf of his lady wife.[75] This theme even appeared in some of the homage scenes directly, reminding us that the process technically represented the couple even when performed by the husband alone.[76] Just as they both relied on each other for access to power, Jeanne and Charles each had a direct source of legitimacy in the form of inheritance and homage respectively. The fact that these neat parallels blurred easily made it important to continually assess the basis of leadership—it was never a settled question—but also provided opportunities to develop the narrative in different ways. In the framework of these relational reputations, legitimacy was transferrable and therefore negotiable, even

68 Amiens, 2:215; Abridged, 131, 409; FrB, 2:151, 6:148.

69 Rome, 494; Amiens, 2:148.

70 Amiens, 2:133–34; cf. Rome, 474.

71 Amiens, 2:131, 133, 145; Rome, 590; cf. Abridged, 417; FrB, 6:162.

72 Amiens, 2:96; FrB, 2:86.

73 Abridged, 112; FrB, 2:305.

74 Amiens, 2:136.

75 FrB, 6:151; Amiens, 3:333.

76 E.g., Amiens, 2:153; Abridged, 119.

though (and perhaps because) it rested on such ostensibly immutable concepts as birthright, marriage, and gender.

Delegated Leadership in Action

If leadership in the Breton civil war began with questions of status and relationships, this authority still had to be put into action to be fully realized. Froissart wondered why Charles did not act faster against Jean de Montfort, a problem that clearly kept bothering him: "what was Charles de Blois thinking, who claimed to have as his wife and spouse the rightful heiress of Brittany, and who was of such great lineage in France, that he did not set forth, but let the count of Montfort do what he liked?"[77] The Breton barons were, he explained, unable to take up his cause on their own, but needed someone to lead them in arms. We can therefore distinguish between lordship in general, and the role of *chef de guerre*, a war leader in a specific conflict.[78] This was by default a male role, so these chivalric chronicles predictably centred on Charles. Nevertheless, Jeanne appeared sporadically at Charles's side, especially when the direction of the conflict was changing, such as rallying troops for a new strategy or confronting a threat of siege.[79] These appearances, entirely absent in Le Bel, emphasized their shared interests and made their partnership integral to the war's narrative as a whole. Going a step further, Froissart appears to have been increasingly interested in the alternation between Jeanne and Charles that marked the two main turning-points in the war: once after his capture at La Roche-Derrien (1347) and again after his death at Auray (1364). The different possibilities for narrating this shifting power show how the mutual dependence established between them produced a complicated process of delegated authority in the management of violence.

To begin in 1347, whereas the Amiens and Abridged chronicles passed over the consequences of Charles's capture in silence (and Cuvelier omitted the capture entirely), Froissart's B version noted that Charles's fortresses and towns continued to hold out because "milady his wife, who called herself duchess of Brittany, took up the war with great will."[80] Her action, Frois-

77 Rome, 474; cf. Amiens, 2:114, 121, 129, 132, 134; Abridged, 112.

78 Cf. Blincoe, "Geoffrey le Bel of Anjou," 91.

79 Amiens, 2:156, 253, 279; Abridged, 119, 144; FrB, 3:17, 6:149; Rome, 557, 573, 579.

80 FrB, 4:43.

sart explained, brought about "the war of these two ladies" (referring to Jeanne de Flandre, countess of Montfort).[81] This brief mention indicated that Jeanne was Charles's deputy: the fortified sites remained his, but she was able to step into his place. Froissart's reminder of Jeanne's claim to the title suggested it was on this basis as much as her marriage that she assumed command. Moreover, he returned to this theme in setting up the chivalric encounter of the Combat of Thirty in 1351, noting that the Breton wars continued "between the parties of the two ladies" in their strongholds.[82] Now Jeanne was fully in charge of her faction, not just a proxy. The 1351 mention also appeared in Amiens and ultimately originated in Le Bel: but in these earlier works it came out of nowhere.[83] By the B version, Froissart had apparently decided the idea of a face-off between the would-be duchesses was important enough to show the transition between Charles and Jeanne as war leader.

Finally, the Rome text elaborated on the consequences of La Roche-Derrien at length:

> The wife of milord Charles de Blois, who was staying at Nantes and who called herself duchess of Brittany, took up the bit in her teeth and showed the heart of a man and of a lion. She kept together all her companions, the knights and squires of her faction, and she made the viscount of Rohan and milord Robert de Beaumanoir captains and overseers of her troops. And when the knights and squires came to her in her service, she showed them two fair sons which she had by milord Charles de Blois her husband, Jean and Guy, and said: "Here are my children and heirs. If their father has done

---

81 In the modern period, this turn of phrase has given rise to the name "War of the Two Jeannes" (*la guerre des deux Jeanne*) as a shorthand for the war of succession. The earliest use I can find is in an early nineteenth-century university textbook (Desmichels, *Tableau chronologique*, 132), where it refers specifically to the war after 1347. The lack of comment or explanation suggests that the designation may already have been current in popular usage, but it does not appear to have been adopted by the major historiographers of Brittany before the twentieth century.

82 FrB, 4:110.

83 Amiens, 3:54; Le Bel, *Chronique*, 2:194. There is also an interesting shift in the terminology of the Combat of Thirty proper, where Jean (here, Robert) de Beaumanoir proposed the fight to the Englishman Robert Bemborough (here, Brandebourch). In Le Bel, Amiens, and the Abridgment (284), he suggested that they fight "for love of their *dames*," the same term for "ladies" that was used in describing the ongoing war. In the B and Rome texts, this word became *amies*, evoking the lady/knight relationship of courtly romance. This sense was perhaps what was also intended in the earlier versions, but given the set-up Froissart felt apparently that further clarity was needed to make sure the combat read as a chivalric more than a political undertaking.

> you well, I and the children will do you even better." And the said lady rode from town to town and from fortress to fortress, those that held for her, revitalizing and encouraging those whom milord Charles de Blois her husband had put and established there. And the lady waged as good and as strong a war against the countess of Montfort and her people, as before milord Charles de Blois and his people had done.[84]

Laying the foundations for the war of the two ladies, this passage mirrored almost word-for-word the countess of Montfort's takeover after her husband's capture and death, a scene originating with Le Bel.[85] Froissart, however, subtly updated his description to reflect the differences in the two Jeannes' positions, emphasizing Jeanne de Penthièvre's place within the ducal line while setting Jeanne de Flandre outside it. He clearly remained sensitive to the specific context of each woman's authority.

Moreover, whereas in the B text Jeanne simply took the lead "with great will," reflecting women's routine seigneurial capacity, in Rome she did so with "the heart of a man and of a lion." This phrasing created a double-gendering: the war of the two ladies ultimately saw them competing in manly terms. Invoking the trope of the virago (which meant literally to act like a man) was, for Froissart, praise for the two Jeannes.[86] At the same time, it underscored the emergency that demanded Jeanne go above and beyond the limits of her usual gendered role. Her newfound masculinity also emphasized that she had not one narrative counterpart, but two: her rival and her husband. Jeanne's ability to wage war was explicitly compared with Charles's several times in this passage, with Jeanne meeting or exceeding the precedents he set as a military leader. Moreover, the power transfer was now immediate: these were her companions, her fortresses, her service, her party, even if they had been initially established by Charles. By detailing how Jeanne assumed leadership from Charles, Froissart further clarified the mechanisms of their joint power. Delegation happened reciprocally. Jeanne assumed her husband's command in his absence, reflecting a widespread expectation that noblewomen should be prepared to assume a masculine role as needed; other writers likewise spoke of such women as having the "heart of a man."[87] But Charles had been Jeanne's delegate in the first place,

---

84 Rome, 817–18.

85 Le Bel, *Chronique,* 1:271–72.

86 Cf. LoPrete, "Gendering Viragos," 21.

87 LoPrete, "Women, Gender and Lordship," esp. 1929; Pizan, *Livre des trois vertus,* 150–51; cf. Westerhof, *Death and the Noble Body*, 42, 51–54.

leading the army to prosecute her claim to the duchy. In his absence, therefore, the role could simply revert to her, and she did not *have* to become masculine to take the war in hand.

These same factors—Jeanne's and Charles's respective contributions, the need for a military leader, and processes of delegation—played out in a different format at the end of the war. This time, Charles was dead, and Froissart seems to have hesitated over the impact of his removal from the field. Lacking Le Bel as a model, he initially focused on Jeanne's strikingly feminine outpouring of sorrow while Jean de Montfort completed his conquest of the duchy. In the Amiens text, King Charles V sent his brother, Louis d'Anjou, to comfort Jeanne (again styled duchess and heiress of Brittany), left abandoned and dismayed by her husband's death and her sons' imprisonment.[88] Even Louis's offer to take over as her war leader (*chiés de le guerre*) did not lift his mother-in-law's spirits. Instead, Jeanne took comfort in her little son Henri, and wept for her lost friends. Tears of grief for the slain were not automatically feminized, but became so when coupled with powerless passivity.[89] It was thus still the "party of Charles de Blois" to whom a few towns stayed loyal.[90] Conversely, Jeanne took positive action in the Abridgement: although still distressed and dismayed, she summoned Louis to help maintain her inheritance, and it was only French intervention that stymied this renewed enterprise.[91] Somewhere between the two, the B version claimed that when King Charles sent Louis to Jeanne, she could not possibly have been more grieving and distressed by her husband's death, but she had confidence in his support until the king changed his mind and sought peace.[92]

All three variations—the incompleteness of Rome is especially regrettable here—suggest that Charles himself was not strictly necessary as a war leader. After all, it was Jeanne's duchy, and if she was willing to go on, so too could the war. Even the *Grandes chroniques*, taking the royal point of view, conceded that Jeanne could have been a plausible rallying point for a Breton resistance had one manifested.[93] Later in Book I, Froissart described how Bertrand du Guesclin waged war in Jeanne's name against

88 Amiens, 3:356.

89 Casey, "Feeling It Like a Man," 237, 243–44, 245.

90 Amiens, 3:358.

91 Abridged, 418.

92 FrB, 6:173.

93 Delachenal, ed., *Grandes chroniques*, 2:6.

English invaders in the viscounty of Limoges to the south, forcing the town of Saint-Yrieix to surrender to Jeanne's obedience.[94] Louis d'Anjou was clearly a plausible substitute for the late duke, especially as Jeanne's son-in-law. Moreover, the events of 1347 had shown that Jeanne could even uphold the fight on her own. What was truly lost with her husband was Charles's connection to French backing. Cuvelier focused on this aspect, highlighting King Charles's grief over his kinsman's death and the end of his alliance with Brittany.[95] The Prose Guesclin B initially painted a similar picture, but added that after the treaty of Guérande (made contrary to the terms consented by Jeanne), Louis offered to champion the rights of his wife and mother-in-law before the king's intervention put an end to the project.[96] Whereas after Charles's capture, Froissart noted that King Philippe continued to send troops to his kinswoman (*cousine*) Jeanne, the refusal to perpetuate this relationship after Charles's demise rendered Jeanne's new delegation of power ineffectual.[97]

The need for a war leader was therefore not strictly a matter of gender. Bertrand du Guesclin had acted in that capacity for Charles de Blois; the Prose Guesclin A even said Bertrand "governed" the war in Brittany on Charles's behalf.[98] Delegation was, after all, a routine part of warfare and of lordship generally. Gendered cues, however, could be deployed to reinforce specific narrative interpretations. Each of Froissart's portrayals of Jeanne's mourning laid more or less stress on her feminine role. The Amiens text went furthest in this direction, highlighting not only her paralysing tears but her position as a mother wrapped up in her (politically irrelevant) youngest child.[99] Her abdication of authority here contrasts oddly with the loyalty she inspired at the start of the war, before Charles stepped into the role of military leader. It was also a far cry from the manly will and courage that let her take command in 1347. These weaker emotions were tempered or quickly overcome in the versions of the story where Jeanne was more active. Masculinity and femininity thus (optionally) heightened the dynamics of delegation within the aristocratic partnership more than they drove them.

94 FrB, 7:248–49.

95 Chanson, ll. 7279–88; PGA, 151.

96 PGB, 27, 29.

97 Rome, 818.

98 FrB, 6:154; PGA, 63.

99 Cf. Boquet and Nagy, *Medieval Sensibilities*, 179–80.

Honour and the Justification of Violence

In these chivalric texts, Charles and Jeanne largely appeared as representatives of their types, that is, as an exemplary nobleman and noblewoman. The inclusion of emotive elements may make them seem more like individuals, but their behaviour was codified to help readers parse the significance of their actions, in keeping with the works' commemorative and didactic aims. Nevertheless, this interpretive process was complicated by Charles's saintly aura as well as the competing demands of knighthood. This time, the problem was less that he had fought, than that he had lost. If defeat did not always threaten knightly honour, it was important to lose for the right reasons.[100] How could Charles's death at Auray be explained as something other than a failure of leadership?

Froissart, Cuvelier, and their adaptors explained the interactions of joint lordship in various ways to give different answers to this question, and so reassessed the gendered dimensions of aristocratic conflict. Craig Taylor points out that because knights and nobles respected the capacity for violence, there are "important and complicated questions regarding the gendering of honour and shame in chivalric culture."[101] Unsurprisingly, the traditional standards for assessing specifically feminine honour relied entirely on non-martial qualities.[102] But if Ruth Mazo Karras has gone so far as to suggest that women could not gain honour within a chivalric framework, Kimberly LoPrete identifies a trickier problem: while women's potential for manly action was praiseworthy, they were still expected to adhere to feminine ideals.[103] As the two norms were not necessarily easy to reconcile, this gap could be exploited to convey moral judgements. Within the dynamics of delegated power, whether violent actions were honourable or not depended on who was doing them and why.

In both full-length versions of Froissart, the preparations for the battle of Auray put a spotlight on the relationship between the duke and duchess. First, Charles assembled the Breton nobles to help him defend his inheritance against his foes. They were willing to serve their lord (by right of his wife) because they had done homage to him. Charles greeted them joyfully and gave them a warm welcome. Then, when it was time to head out,

100 Karras, *From Boys to Men*, 24, 40, 60.

101 Taylor, *Chivalry and the Ideals of Knighthood*, 70 and n. 101.

102 Crouch, *Chivalric Turn*, chaps. 5 and 8.

103 Karras, *From Boys to Men*, 28, 60; LoPrete, "Gendering Viragos," 21.

> they took leave of milady the wife of milord Charles de Blois, who gave it to them gladly and said to her husband with the barons of Brittany present: "My lord, you are going to defend and preserve my inheritance and yours, for what is mine is yours. In this, Sir Jean de Montfort impedes us, and has long impeded us, wrongly and without cause—as God knows, and these barons of Brittany—even though I am the rightful heiress. So I pray you dearly that you commit to no arrangement, accord or treaty by which the whole of the duchy does not remain ours." And the knight Sir Charles de Blois promised her that he would not do this. So he kissed her and took his leave, and the lady most pleasantly gave it to him and to all the barons of Brittany too, one after the other.[104]

This scene drew attention to all the salient features of mutually delegated ducal authority we saw above. The inheritance was transferable from wife to husband (though this needed to be pointed out explicitly), and their interests aligned on the basis of this shared possession. In the Amiens text quoted here, Jeanne was nevertheless repeatedly recognized as the source of that authority, while Charles was legitimized by his ties of homage. Conversely, the B version initially downplayed both Jeanne's claim and Charles's personal connections to create a more homogenous lordship. Yet it also added a final detail that the lords "took leave of their lady, whom they held as duchess," achieving a similar effect. This pattern echoed the captains who had originally held out against the senior Jean de Montfort in Jeanne's name at the start of the war, although Jeanne now directly dictated the terms on which battle might be avoided.

This scene established that Charles led the army in person, but he and his followers ultimately acted on Jeanne's behalf, not just his own. The duke both commanded and served, while the duchess pursued the war but only by proxy. Amiens in particular evoked certain tropes of courtly gender dynamics to reinforce these interactions. The leave-taking itself was a formal ritual repeatedly reflected in contemporary literature, and here served to publicly place Jeanne's trust in her husband and the knights who followed them.[105] Her gracious manners and Charles's farewell kiss (omitted in B) played up the image of knightly service to a lady.[106] At the same time, the sentiments and actions displayed here were part of a wider performance of leadership undertaken by men as well as

104 Amiens, 3:333–34; cf. FrB, 6:151–52.

105 Burnley, *Courtliness and Literature*, 57–58.

106 Carré, *Baiser*, 66; Karras, *From Boys to Men*, 25, 61.

women.[107] Charles's warm welcome to his troops was couched in the same emotional terms as Jeanne's farewell: both spoke *liement*—joyfully or gladly—with their troops. Earlier in the war, the Rome text showed Charles thanking his men for their service, receiving them "most gladly one after the other," just as Jeanne did in 1364.[108] Meanwhile, although the B version removed the emotive reactions of both Jeanne and Charles in the leave-taking, it had them jointly greet Bertrand du Guesclin "gladly [*liement*] and gently [*doucement*]" at Nantes just before they made the decision to fight at Auray.[109] Once on the battlefield itself, Charles would again "most pleasingly and gently" or "most gladly and gently" exhort his troops to their best efforts.[110] Courteous, individualized interactions were a core component of the affective side of military leadership, regardless of gender.[111] Moreover, historians of emotions have come to recognize how "emotional communities" structure affective relationships within different social groups and shape how these ties are supposed to be expressed, both personally and rhetorically.[112] This leave-taking connected both the duke and the duchess to the same elite, martial community.

Even the power dynamics and connotations of the kiss were more complicated than they might first appear, since this gesture was used not only in romantic contexts, but as a political gesture of friendship and trust. Most notably, it was a traditional part of the homage ceremony wherein a subordinate pledged loyalty to their superior. The implications of performing such a ritual public kiss between men and women were repeatedly debated due to concerns over sexual propriety and gendered hierarchies.[113]

---

107 Boquet and Nagy, *Medieval Sensibilities*, 105, speak of the "reasoned use of the emotions in the exercise of power"; cf. 158–59, 177–78, 180, on the importance of emotions to late medieval political history. On the ritualization and even institutionalization of emotional performance in the service of socio-political order, see Rosenwein, "Thinking Historically," 830–31.

108 Rome, 590.

109 FrB, 6:149.

110 FrB, 6:154; Amiens, 3:337.

111 Cf. Pizan, *Livre des trois vertus*, 150–51; Wittig, *Learning to Be Noble*, 134; Karras, *From Boys to Men*, 25, 46; Boquet and Nagy, *Medieval Sensibilities*, 104.

112 Rosenwein, "Thinking Historically," 832; Rosenwein, *Emotional Communities*, introduction, and esp. 25–29 on the mediating role of texts; cf. Broomhall, "Introduction," 1.

113 Major, "'Bastard Feudalism' and the Kiss," 514–15, 517–18, 521; Carré, *Baiser*, 109, 203–4.

However, the gesture made clear sense here both as a sentimental exchange between spouses and as a representation of Jeanne's delegation of power to Charles, since it parallelled a vassal's kiss to their lord.[114] The emotions and rituals in this scene differentiated Jeanne and Charles while confirming them both in their authority.

Charles's image of cheerful lordship is particularly striking because the canonization trial had stressed his sober and pious temperament to appeal to the emotional values of the Church. But his affability also translated across the (admittedly porous) boundaries between the clerical and aristocratic emotional communities by aligning with each group's priorities. During the papal inquiry, Charles's kindness to his subordinates, including his martial followers, had substantiated claims of his humility.[115] Now, they made good military sense. For example, Charles consulted with the castellan or captain of the besieged city to encourage him to hold out, receiving him gladly (*liement*), joyfully (*joieusement*), or even laughing aloud (*tout en riant*).[116] Although most contemporary readers would have known the tragic outcome of Auray—a dramatic irony Froissart surely intended—Charles's almost relentlessly positive attitude, associated as it was with knightly honour, was an essential part of encouraging his troops and retaining their loyalty.[117] Similarly, if his performance of religious rites before battle or tendency to give credit to God had been used in 1371 to show he prioritized spiritual over worldly matters, they were also a necessary part of a leader's attention to their army's well-being.[118] The performance of piety and chivalry were acceptable as two sides of the same coin.

Elsewhere we find sharper shifts in the emotional reputation, so to speak, that legitimized Charles's leadership in this new phase. As a knight and prince he was allowed displays of strong and even violent feeling that he had not shown as a saint.[119] The squire Jean de Plessey, among others, reported in 1371 that whenever Charles learned of the capture of his castles

---

114 Carré, *Baiser*, 68, 108, 140–43, 190, 192, 196, 208, 209.

115 E.g., D31.2, 38.2, 49.2.

116 Amiens, 3:340; Abridged, 411; FrB, 6:158.

117 White, "Politics of Anger," 142–43.

118 E.g., Amiens, 3:342–43; Abridged, 411; FrB, 6:159.

119 Karras, *From Boys to Men*, 65–65; Boquet and Nagy, *Medieval Sensibilities*, 169–71; Broomhall, "Introduction," 4; though cf. White, "Politics of Anger," 149, on angry saints.

or the death of his warriors, he never became angry.[120] To be sure, this calmness was also evidence of the manly self-restraint needed for governance. But especially within the courtly and chivalric community, it became acceptable to express righteous anger in the defence of personal honour and rightful seigneurial authority.[121] In the Rome manuscript, when Charles heard the town of Carhaix had defected, he "was greatly angered" and swore on the spot to besiege it.[122] The loss of La Roche-Derrien in 1347 provoked a similar reaction, as Charles vowed to retake it at once no matter the cost, punish those responsible, and exact "such a harsh vengeance that it would be an example to all others."[123] This violent lordship could not contrast more starkly with Charles's lordly priorities at the siege of Quimper, where the witnesses had instead emphasized his protective measures. Froissart now described the duke's determination to seize the castle of Jugon as his troops took whatever supplies they could from the town's inhabitants.[124] In the Rome text, Charles ordered his men to restore what they had taken, but enforced it poorly; and while he let residents peacefully take refuge in the castle, it was merely a tactic to overload the defenders' supplies.[125] In the Amiens text, he was reluctant to give the town of Vannes a respite from assault, and had to be persuaded by his barons that it was better to conquer through love than hate.[126] Mercy was certainly a chivalric virtue, but the demands of war could override such concerns.[127] Meanwhile for Cuvelier, Charles enjoyed fighting: a man of valiant courage, he came to Auray gladly (*lyement* again) and bore himself fiercely (*fierement*) into battle.[128] These emotional attributes signalled Charles's effectiveness as a knight and lord, but would have been out of place before the papal curia.

Nevertheless, the canonization process took place before either Cuvelier or Froissart set pen to parchment, and it had consequences for the historiographers. If Froissart's earliest text (Amiens) did not refer to Charles's holiness, the next stressed the point in some detail. Buried reverently at

120 D41.7.

121 White, "Politics of Anger," 143–45; Barton, "'Zealous Anger,'" 154, 155.

122 Rome, 557.

123 Rome, 812; cf. Amiens, 3:42; Abridged, 244; FrB, 4:40.

124 FrB, 2:180.

125 Rome, 559–60.

126 Amiens, 2:226.

127 Taylor, *Chivalry and the Ideals of Knighthood*, chap. 6.

128 Chanson, ll. 6748, 6804, 6813.

Guingamp, Charles's body was sanctified by God's grace, and "they call him Saint Charles, whom Pope Urban V approved and canonized."[129] This version's wide circulation would have promoted its interpretation. Two iterations of Book III also experimented in summarizing the Breton war. Whereas the version written around 1390–1391 consistently spoke of "Sir [*messire*] Charles de Blois" as usual, a later revision called him "Saint Charles de Blois" instead.[130] Cuvelier likewise reported that "they say and believe truly that he's a saint," and added a miracle where Charles healed a soldier driven mad after boasting of having killed the duke.[131] The premise was adopted by the Prose Guesclin A, if with slightly greater restraint.[132] Charles's holy reputation was progressively integrated into the chivalric discourse.

The Prose Guesclin B offers a point of comparison for how specific details of Charles's sanctity did (or did not) circulate in French circles. On one hand, the strict imprisonment that some canonization witnesses had linked to Charles's increasing asceticism was a far cry from later descriptions of his captivity. Le Bel merely stated how long his ransom took.[133] The B version went further: although Charles was initially placed in "courteous imprisonment" along with the king of Scotland and the earl of Moray, Queen Philippa quickly intervened on her cousin's behalf to allow him out on parole around London for up to a night at a time, or more if Charles was in the company of herself or the king.[134] The Rome manuscript even claimed that Charles played boardgames with his fellow prisoners, attended a royal party, flew falcons, and went sparring in the countryside whenever he wanted, so long as he checked in every fifth day.[135] Never, the text specified, was he put in confinement. This environment was hardly one for penitential reflection. On the other hand, there are clear indications that stories of Charles's suffering at the battle itself circulated in French political society. The Prose Guesclin B unsurprisingly added the episode of Charles's capture, which Cuvelier and the Prose A had skipped over.[136] It reported that he

129 FrB, 6:171.

130 Besançon, BM, MS 865, fols. 309r–310v; Paris, Bibliothèque nationale de France (BnF), MS français 2650, fols. 152v–154r.

131 Chanson, ll. 2466, 7357–75; cf. 3462–64.

132 PGA, 71, 152.

133 Le Bel, *Chronique,* 2:149.

134 FrB, 4:66–67.

135 Rome, 819, 875–76.

136 PGB, 7.

received seventeen mortal wounds, a number reduced (intentionally or by scribal error) to seven in the *Grandes chroniques*, but tallying exactly with what Charles's physician Georges de Lesnen reported in 1371.[137] It likewise added that the Englishman Thomas Dagworth shut Charles naked in a cellar with only a bit of straw to lie on, a streamlined and dramatized reworking of another part of Georges's testimony. A garbled version of this story made it into Froissart's Rome text, which told how the English rescued a captive Thomas Dagworth who lay wounded on a mattress in Charles's tent.[138] The parallels with the canonization underscored the value placed by the Penthièvre family on Georges's testimony, and it is possible he spread these recollections himself thereafter.[139] Still, the uneven success of such anecdotes in shaping the wider chronicle discourse suggests that Charles's life as a saint was not usually the historiographers' highest priority.

Instead, his sanctity mattered most when it came to interpreting his death—which now had to be justified from a chivalric perspective too. The Prose Guesclin B went so far as to insert a synopsis of Charles's character at the end of his life. This eulogy mirrored the canonization tactics of combining a princely exterior with a saintly interior, but also laid greater stress on Charles's chivalric prowess. It reported that Charles had won sixteen of his eighteen battles and that he was "the fairest knight of France and the most endowed with valour, doing only that which pertains to a prince, for there was never a battle in which he did not wish to be out in front, and many times he was the first to fall upon his enemies."[140] Indeed, at Auray Charles had overruled his knights to take personal command of the first battalion.[141] Far from a reluctant duke, Charles's behaviour was exemplary for his status, standing out not for his temperance but for being the most agreeable and merry (*joly*) of all. He was, moreover, a composer of songs and lays, the latter indubitably secular material, which the *Grandes chroniques de France* apparently corroborated with a curious mention of Charles joining in on the gittern (an instrument similar to a lute or guitar) with other prisoners en route

137 Viard, ed., *Grandes chroniques*, 9:304.

138 Rome, 817.

139 Georges was still alive in 1381, and as master of the cathedral school at Nantes would have had contact with both lay and secular elites: Héry et al., eds., *Procès de canonisation*, 87n82.

140 PGB, 27.

141 PGB, 24.

to England.[142] By contrast, the canonization had naturally focused only on Charles's performance of sacred music alongside his priests.[143] In the chivalric tradition, Charles could be a model *prudhomme*, with consummate manners as well as prowess, and so undisputably virtuous along secular lines.[144]

However, the Prose Guesclin B also reported that Charles covertly led a holy life, as was now borne out by the miracles he performed. Like Cuvelier's original, it described how Charles's corpse was discovered wearing a hairshirt, publicly revealing his inner sanctity after his death in knightly service.[145] This imagery contrasted sharply with Froissart's descriptions of Charles lying dead beneath his shield or upon his axe and surrounded by the bodies of his attackers.[146] He commended Charles as "an especially good knight who valiantly and boldly fought and attacked his foes with great will," and who died with his face towards his enemies.[147] Still, such praise was not meant to contradict Charles's sanctity. Froissart even suggested it was because Charles died valiantly while defending his inheritance that he could be proclaimed a martyr.[148] Charles's spiritual legitimacy continued to derive from his seigneurial legitimacy.

But if this was, in Froissart's estimation, a good death, it was nonetheless a defeat, raising the question: how could a paragon of knighthood and holiness lose? Any possible answer, for these historiographers, depended on another question: should Charles have fought at all? The possibility of a negotiated settlement was first explored at the Landes d'Évran on July 24, 1363. Cuvelier succinctly summarized the preliminary accord: both would-be dukes should receive enough of the duchy's towns to let them each use the title.[149] Froissart moved this compromise to Auray, where the encounter between the two armies was postponed by a last-minute diplomatic effort

---

142 Viard, ed., *Grandes chroniques*, 9:305.

143 E.g., D33.3.

144 Wittig, *Learning to Be Noble*, 159.

145 PGB, 27; Chanson, ll. 7254–55; PGA, 150. The Prose Guesclin B added that his naked body was borne away from the battlefield by a Franciscan monk, Raoul de Carquignolles, perhaps echoing the story of the Dominican who claimed in 1371 to have rescued the discarded hairshirt (D30.8).

146 FrB, 6:171, Amiens, 3:351.

147 FrB, 6:164, 168; Amiens, 3:346, 348.

148 Abridged, 417.

149 Chanson, ll. 3254–63; cf. PGA, 66.

by Jean, lord of Beaumanoir.[150] The chroniclers disagreed on whether this would have been an acceptable solution, and if so, who to blame for its falling through. Cuvelier mused that such a peace may have been fundamentally unobtainable in the long run, leaving battle as the only solution to two intractable claims.[151] Froissart attributed the treaty's failure to the English, and specifically the duplicity of the knight John Chandos. Since his troops opposed the loss of profits they would face in the event of peace, Chandos informed Jean de Beaumanoir that Jean de Montfort was unwilling to accept any partial title to the duchy, before reporting back to his commander, expressly to provoke him, that Charles was determined not to bargain. The Abridgement even stressed the young count of Montfort's eagerness for a peaceful resolution (which here involved some of the real terms from the first treaty of Guérande in 1365), heightening the pathos of the missed opportunity for reconciliation. The possibility of *refraining* from violence was clearly on the table as an honourable option.

The Prose Guesclin B was more militant, embracing the justness of Charles's cause. It preferred not to excuse the count for the breakdown of negotiations, citing his subsequent failure to show up at the bargaining table to finalize the details.[152] Jean was also unreasonable to expect any concessions from the true claimant. This narrative notoriously introduced a new explanation for how Charles died, building on a rumour that had apparently begun circulating soon after the battle.[153] Rather than being killed outright in the melee, he was severely wounded, captured, and brought before his rival. There, Jean de Montfort berated him, accusing him of having fought despite having no right to the duchy: "you are descended of neither the [coat of] arms nor the lineage [of Brittany]." He addressed Charles as the informal *tu* rather than formal *vous*, the pronoun rudely implying Charles's inferiority, and demanded that he renounce his claim on pain of death.[154] Charles responded at length, refuting Jean's own familial claim using the same spurious genealogy (with an extra dose of scandalous adultery) accepted by Froissart, while denying that he, Charles, fought for his own sake: "for you well know that the duchy belongs to my wife and to my children, and not to

150 Amiens, 3:341–43; Abridged, 412–13; FrB, 6:158–62.

151 Chanson, ll. 6241–42, 6272–73.

152 PGB, 14.

153 PGB, 26–27; D9.15.

154 By contrast, in the canonization trial Charles's humility had been exemplified by his use of *vous* towards his own servants.

me, who must defend and uphold their rights, and who cannot give away any part of that which belongs to another." So Jean had one of his men slit Charles's throat in cold blood.[155]

This exchange exposed a potential vulnerability that came with casting Charles as the sole leader of his party, for indeed he had no birthright of his own. But it also revealed the solution to this challenge, which was to remove his agency. Conforming to the expectations of aristocratic bloodlines, he could only implement Jeanne's will, not make decisions for her. Honour was here satisfied by the knightly ideal of service. Moreover, Charles's chivalrous behaviour contrasted with how Jean fell short of that standard, delegitimizing the Montfortist victory. This reasoning brings us back to Jeanne's speech before Auray as recounted by Froissart, where she exercised her right to set limitations on her husband's diplomatic strategy. Similarly, when Jean de Montfort renewed the offer of splitting the duchy on the eve of battle in the Prose Guesclin B (again invoking certain terms of the actual treaty of Guérande), Charles forwarded the proposal to his wife the duchess, she being the one in the line of succession. She, with great mettle, refused the compromise point blank.[156] A woman could legitimately pursue a course of war to defend her seigneurial prerogatives.

But although Jeanne's resolve could be presented positively, it also opened the door to another, more critical interpretation. Four fifteenth-century Froissart manuscripts had an alternative take on Charles's departure for Auray.[157] The first was produced around 1410–1415 by four scribes, one named Raoul Tainguy and three anonymous. Tainguy, a Breton working in Paris, is noteworthy for his "bold" interpolations in the texts he copied, especially concerning affairs of his homeland.[158] Although the relevant passage was transcribed by Tainguy's primary anonymous collaborator, this emendation fits the same pattern. Having left with his army, Charles reflected upon the burden now facing him. The duke "was very gentle and most courteous, [and] would have willingly agreed to peace and been content with only a portion of Brittany with little dispute." Unfortunately, he was "so put upon by his wife and the knights on his side, that he could not

155 The political ramifications of this accusation of murder remained apparent for some time to come: Estourbeillon, *Serment de Jean de Lesnerac*, esp. 7–8.

156 PGB, 23.

157 Luce classified these as the third family of the A redaction: Froissart, *Chroniques*, ed. Luce, 1:xxxiv; Paris, BnF, MS français 2640, fol. 246r; Croenen, "Paris, Bibliothèque nationale"; Tesnière, "Manuscrits copiés par Raoul Tainguy," 352–54.

158 Luce, *France pendant la guerre*, 248–49.

disagree or ignore it."[159] This addition fundamentally altered the dynamics of the ducal couple. Charles was once again a would-be peacetime ruler, but was thwarted in this laudable intention by the bad counsel spearheaded by his wife. The opposition between knight- and sainthood used during the canonization not only reemerged, but now made the duchess in particular shoulder the blame in order exonerate her husband.

This interpretation seems to have been mainly Cuvelier's work in the first instance.[160] Although he implied a decisive combat was inevitable, it was not desired by either pretender if an alternative could be found.[161] Jean de Montfort declared himself willing to settle for half if Charles would allow him, and Chandos even encouraged this offer. Charles, meanwhile, would gladly have granted the request immediately for the honour of God and to end the costly war. Both men were troubled by the spiritual implications of the battle. It was not dear to Jesus, mused Jean de Montfort, while Charles told his companions that he was greatly displeased at the prospect of fighting and the death of good men on his account, which might constitute a sin. Whereas Froissart had Charles stake his soul and his place in Paradise on the righteousness of their cause, in the Cuvelier tradition the demands of Charles's secular station were once again at odds with his spiritual stance.[162] The Prose Guesclin A showed Charles struggling to balance his desire that God aid his pursuit of what he believed a rightful claim, with the burden of moral responsibility.[163] Ultimately, it was his barons who swayed the reluctant Charles. In their judgement, he could only be blamed for *not* attempting to take control of the duchy. They urged Charles to act like a duke: he could not let his inheritance escape him or show fear before one of lower status like Jean de Montfort.[164] Since chivalric honour was determined by one's fellow knights, it was important for Charles to maintain their good opinion.[165]

But where the barons stressed Charles's need to uphold his status as a duke and highborn prince, the focus on Jeanne's inheritance brought the

---

159 FrB, 6:327.

160 The poet himself attributed his account to an unnamed written source (l. 6469), but this claim was likely a move to lend credibility to public rumour or simply introduced for the sake of a rhyme. Raoul Tainguy's close connections to the French court could in turn have facilitated his workshop's access to Cuvelier's poem.

161 Chanson, ll. 6367–72, 6404, 6430–32, 6466–68.

162 FrB, 6:154.

163 PGA, 132.

164 Chanson, ll. 6421–27, 6478–91; PGA, 134.

165 Taylor, *Chivalry and the Ideals of Knighthood*, 57.

issues of knightly service and of shared power to the fore. Charles's desire for a peaceful settlement was rebuked in no uncertain terms:

> it was forcefully said to him, off to one side, "Lord, what are you thinking? For the love of God, you have not the heart of a powerful knight if you wish to give away the rightful inheritance of your pleasant wife like a coward! A knight should in no way hold a land if he does not wish to defend it with sharpened blade."[166]

Though this tirade was presumably delivered by the knights on hand, they were elided from the scene; instead, this speech was made "on behalf of his wife" (*de par sa moillier*). It was irrelevant whether this response came from Jeanne herself—a reading early modern historians certainly embraced—or if it was merely an obvious concern for the Breton lords to raise.[167] Her interests were represented either way, and they took on an aggressively gendered tone. Being unable to defend what belonged to his wife (or to him via her) viscerally threatened Charles's manliness, while Jeanne's anger, her own or by proxy, underscored the risk by potentially making the wife more assertive than her husband.

So while Jeanne gave Charles the impetus to fulfill his secular responsibilities, her forcefulness also made her conveniently culpable for the consequences. She violated gendered hierarchies by demanding battle and commanding her husband. We come back, then, to the reworked farewell speech in Froissart, which had all the markings of an intercession gone wrong. Intercession, particularly as performed by medieval queens, was a popular political tool to let a male ruler exercise mercy or simply change his mind without looking weak, because he did so as a special favour to his spouse. Calling on his softer side with a submissive feminine voice, she allowed a safe exception to the masculine expression of authority and violence.[168] This model for queenly action had biblical precedent in the Virgin Mary and Queen Esther, and tied in with wider expectations of women as peacemakers.[169] Froissart himself composed a classic example of such a scene, where Philippa of Hainault tearfully begged her husband Edward III to spare the lives of six Calais townsmen after the 1346–1347 siege. The king declared himself reluctant to give in, but avoided the charge of cruelty thanks to Philippa's interven-

---

166 Chanson, ll. 6469–76; PGA, 133.

167 Argentré, *Histoire de Bretaigne*, 473.

168 Parsons, "Queen's Intercession," 147; Strohm, *Hochon's Arrow*, 103–4.

169 Parsons, "Queen's Intercession," 153–57, 159; Adams, *Life and Afterlife*, 77; Strohm, *Hochon's Arrow*, 96–98; Huneycutt, "Intercession."

tion.[170] Under Cuvelier's influence, Charles's leave-taking inverted these dynamics: though personally inclined to peace, he was compelled to obey his wife and the knights whom she had functionally co-opted for the pursuit of war. The verb used for their influence, *bouter*, had strong connotations of physical force, such as striking, pushing or thrusting (including in a sexual sense); Froissart used it elsewhere for more- or less-legitimate reversals of position, such as driving out invaders or Jean de Montfort's attempt to evict Jeanne from her inheritance.[171] If the war had presented a challenge during Charles's canonization process, it could likewise interfere with Jeanne's potential to live up to feminine ideals. She had already served as the counterpart to Charles's spiritual extravagance in the curial testimony; now her failings were narratively useful to preserve Charles's honour in the framework of shared power.

After all, the threat to the duke's masculinity was not ultimately realized, for Charles died heroically on the battlefield in service of a worthy enterprise. Cuvelier did not go so far as the Prose Guesclin B in framing Charles's death as an assassination, but he cast moral judgement on the killing: "his banner was thrown to the ground savagely, and Charles brought down and wounded savagely, taken by the helmet and dragged savagely; and there an Englishman, acting perfidiously, put a dagger through his throat so that it came through half a foot on the other side."[172] The rhythmic repetition of the word *laidement*, which I have translated "savagely" for its implications of both violence and the dishonourable tactics used by the false Englishman, very effectively hammered home the shameful brutality of Charles's killers.[173] Cuvelier then concluded that Charles was "so superlative, the most honourable man who ever lived. He always waged war reluctantly and under pressure."[174] The duke's death was laudable precisely because the cause had not been his own.

This point was so important that Cuvelier undercut the immediacy of the duke's death-scene by having Charles deliver some implausible final words. Asking God's forgiveness for the death of his men, he excused himself by saying, "'I have long fought, against my conscience—he who believes his wife too much will repent it in the end!'"[175] The Prose Guesclin A went further,

170 FrB, 4:60–62; Benz St. John, *Three Medieval Queens*, 53–54.

171 Amiens, 3:358; Rome, 463.

172 Chanson, ll. 7152–57.

173 Cf. Karras, *From Boys to Men*, 38–39.

174 Chanson, ll. 7169–71; PGA, 14[8].

175 Chanson, ll. 7163–64.

having Charles explain (despite having been stabbed through the mouth) that he had fought, unwillingly, "'through the instigation of my wife, who always led me to believe that I was completely in the right.'"[176] Not only did this framing move from the trite misogyny of an adage to a more concrete context, it cast Jeanne's claim as deliberately manipulative. The word *en(n) ortement*, meaning instigation or advice, appeared repeatedly as an excuse in contemporary pardon letters, often implying an unequal or subversive power balance. Jeanne's duplicity regarding her claims was also hinted at in the poem, where Charles explained to his men that "'I believe that I have the right to this lordship and that, for my wife whom I love blamelessly, I must bear its name without falseness.'"[177] Invoking the vocabulary of knightly service to women, Charles's actions were faultless because Jeanne's were not. The persuasiveness of this trope relied on established notions of the perversity of women, but at root Charles's problem, and Jeanne's, was the corruption of order. Contemporary expectations held that noblewomen and queens should above all practice submission to their husband and work towards peace and mediation, while kings who fell too much under the control of their wives (or mothers) were liable to be led astray.[178] In a traditional intercession, the wife's feminine leniency allowed her husband to relax his hypermasculinity in the service of good rule. Here, her transgression of these standards justified his saintly inclinations towards peace.

The ducal couple laid bare the inconsistencies of achieving chivalric honour through the pursuit of violence. Charles was a worthy knight, even a saint, for dying in defence of his seigneurial rights and service to his lady. Jeanne, too, could be honoured for refusing to compromise her lawful inheritance and pursuing war towards this end. Both of them communicated the affective aspects of martial leadership and connected with the knightly community in similar ways. However, Jeanne was vulnerable to a less charitable reading that saw her warmongering as disruptive. As heiress, she could not fall back on her marriage to excuse any self-serving actions, unlike Jeanne de Flandre, who was praised for fighting for her husband's cause (effectively giving her access to the honour of knightly service). Jeanne's exclusion from the chivalric ideal was not an automatic outcome of gendered principles, but

176 PGA, 14[8].

177 Chanson, ll. 6326–28.

178 Allirot, "*Male royne boiteuse*," 128–30; Turner, "Eleanor of Aquitaine," 24, 26, 28; Marvin, "Regicidal Queens," 167; Huneycutt, "Creation of a Crone," 34.

a constructed tension that linked the structures of shared power to the justification for conflict.

Conclusions

The fluid development of these chivalric reputations showcases some of the possibilities for how aristocratic audiences interpreted shared power as part of a politically charged discourse. Legitimate authority was partly a function of networking, both within the bounds of the marriage partnership itself and in the wider context of family, friends, and followers (to borrow Gerd Althoff's famous formulation).[179] These connections permitted a flexible interpretation of the demands of military leadership as the war progressed, as processes of mutual delegation mitigated moments of acute pressure. At the same time, because chivalric legitimacy and honour were evaluated at once on an individual and a collective basis, there were limits to how far an aristocratic couple was interchangeable. Gendered differences, in particular, could be used to underline both continuities and disruptions in the provision of leadership, and so helped turn the events of the contested succession into the story of a war. Jeanne and Charles continued to be seen as both partners and counterparts, as they had been during the canonization and would continue to be under the Montfortist chroniclers to whom I turn next.

This interplay of honourable violence, gender norms, and power-sharing adds further dimensions to understanding leadership in the framework of constant crisis. As Michel Nassiet, among others, has observed, disputes were likely to flare up when women stood to inherit powerful territories (as they regularly did).[180] This potential for turbulence can therefore be seen as a normal part of these women's subsequent authority, which was both routinely accepted and routinely disrupted. Strife, in other words, did not delegitimize their role. Nor were their fights necessarily distinct from those in which all nobles might expect to participate simply by virtue of being part of the aristocracy, with its cultures of status competition and martial power. These social relationships, predicated on the possibility of violence, continually both drove and resolved conflicts. The co-participation of both chivalric men and, if we may go so far, chivalric women in this value system helped make late medieval politics what it was.

179 Althoff, *Family, Friends and Followers.*

180 Nassiet, *Parenté*, 197–98; Wolf, "Reigning Queens"; Waag, "Rulership, Authority, and Power."

Chapter 3

DYNASTIC DIVISIONS

THE LATER FIFTEENTH century saw the Montfort dynasty confronting its own succession troubles. They had run out of male heirs and the potential claim of Jeanne and Charles's descendants was enshrined in the treaties of Guérande. Tensions were exacerbated by renewed conflict with France under the regency of Anne de Beaujeu. The eventual resolution came with the advent of Duchess Anne (r. 1488–1514), who was also twice queen of France thanks to her marriages to Charles VIII (r. 1483–1498) in 1491 and to Louis XII (r. 1498–1515) in 1499. Despite rocky beginnings, Anne's rule came to mark a period of political and cultural productivity for the duchy even as it slowly shifted course towards unification with the kingdom (1532).[1] In the face of internal uncertainty alongside external threats (or opportunities, depending on one's point of view), the official ducal histories of this period consolidated patriotic sentiment and exalted the duchess's lineage. In so doing, they drew on the earlier chivalric chronicles as well as a regional tradition of history-writing within the inner Montfortist circles, offering a re-evaluation of the civil war from the other side, so to speak.

It is in this phase of reputational development that we might expect elements of a so-called "black legend" to develop around the Penthièvre leaders. Women rulers were perennially at risk of slander that sought to undermine their authority by portraying them as inadequately performing their feminine roles, attempting to undeservedly perform a masculine role, or both. While specific examples will be cited below, it is telling that all but two of the chapters in the most recent volume on queenly reputations focus on the negative portrayal of their subjects.[2] In the case of male rulers, as we have seen, it was more likely for blame to be deflected to those around them, but they too could be attacked for failing as men or abusing their power. The Montfortist historiography, however, engaged only superficially with such motifs, and it is worth examining why their impact remained limited on the winning side of the war. I consider in turn

1 Brown, *Cultural and Political Legacy*.

2 Rohr and Benz, *Queenship, Gender, and Reputation*; cf. Graham-Goering, "Authority," 100–101.

the negative tropes that were retained or developed here, as well as those that could have appeared but did not. There were even positive portrayals of both Jeanne and Charles in these accounts, which attest the ongoing weighing of reputational alternatives.

Although much of this material was drawn from previous narratives, the gendering of Jeanne's and Charles's leadership responded to new political demands and the reconceptualization of ducal authority. Understanding the civil war through the lens of aristocratic partnership helped these authors overcome the contradictions in their stance on female succession. At the same time, Jeanne's and Charles's relational reputations became more independent of each other than in previous phases, reflecting the plasticity of the familial and lineal identities that lay at the heart of aristocratic legitimacy. Treating them separately helped communicate the "correct" interpretation of Breton history within a dynastic framework, of the sort that increasingly characterizes the study of early modern polities in particular.[3] Nevertheless, approving or condemning one half of a ruling couple did not undermine the sharing of power itself, which points towards the conceptual resilience of the practice of co-rule.

Reputation in Ducal Historiography

The two writers at the centre of this chapter are Pierre Le Baud (1458–1505) and Alain Bouchart (d. by 1531).[4] Both came from noble families in western Brittany and played a role in the ducal administration, especially under Duchess Anne, although Le Baud was a churchman by training and Bouchart a lawyer. Their careers shaped their history-writing in two similar ways. First, they both took what we might call a technical approach to their narratives of the civil war, engaging with more of the legal details surrounding the original succession dispute and its various settlements, as well as the genealogies of the people involved. When using older accounts, they were critical of the material they repeated or adapted, evaluating its reliability, comparing different versions, and correcting errors.[5] Second, putting the record straight (as they saw it) served the interests not only of

3 Backerra, "Personal Union"; Brero et al., "Dynasties and Dynastic Rule," 43–44; Watts, "Lordship and the State," 24–25.

4 The editions of their works used here are Le Baud, *Compillation* (hereafter LBC); Le Baud, "'*Genealogie*'" (hereafter LBG); Le Baud, *Histoire* (hereafter LBH); Bouchart, *Grandes croniques* (hereafter GCB).

5 Cassard, "Historien au travail."

their successive patrons, but their own in the fate of the Montfortist duchy. Anne's succession was a politically delicate moment, not entirely unlike that of Duchess Jeanne's some hundred and forty years earlier. Le Baud and Bouchart responded to these tensions with a dynastically oriented attempt to put Brittany and its dukes on a solid historical footing in relation to their powerful French neighbour.

Pierre Le Baud was the more prolific, though at the same time less publicly successful, of the two authors. His successive employers determined the shape of his historiographical output. He first secured the patronage of the powerful Laval and Derval families, to whom he was related on his mother's side. As secretary to Jean de Derval, Le Baud was commissioned to write a "Compilation of the chronicles and histories of the Bretons," probably around 1470–1473.[6] One of the nine great barons of Brittany, Jean was also a prolific book collector, and Le Baud likely had access to his extensive library. As suggested by its name, the *Compillation* synthesized other texts such as Froissart, whose popularity boomed in this period, and the *Grandes chroniques de France*.[7] Jean de Derval had copies of both these works, though the inclusion of certain anecdotes suggests that Le Baud may have consulted several versions of Froissart.[8] He also used classical authorities such as Lucan to place the destiny of the Breton people on par with the supposed great civilizations.[9] This first version of his work survives, however, in only two manuscripts, suggesting a limited audience beyond its original patron.

Le Baud then became almoner to Francois II's wife, Marguerite de Foix, for whom he composed a brief genealogy of the kings and dukes of Brittany just before her death in 1486. This work served as both an overview of ducal history for Marguerite (who came from what is now southern France, though she had by then lived in Brittany for fifteen years) and, above all, to defend women's succession to the duchy in light of the probable claim of Marguerite's daughter Anne.[10] The need to reconcile female inheritance with the legitimacy of the Montfort line posed a real problem for the late Montfortist historians, as I will discuss further, and this short piece had slightly more uptake than the voluminous *Compillation*, with four extant manuscripts,

6 Le Baud, *Compillation*, ed. Abélard, 10.

7 Tesnière, "Manuscrits copiés par Raoul Tainguy," 302.

8 Le Baud, *Compillation*, ed. Abélard, 13.

9 Le Baud, *Compillation*, ed. Abélard, 16 (cf. 395), 22.

10 Le Baud, "'*Genealogie*,'" ed. Kerhervé, 519.

two of them apparently practical working copies.[11] Finally, Le Baud became priest and councillor to Duchess Anne herself, for whom he reworked his *Compillation* into a more streamlined "Book of the chronicles of the kings, dukes, and royal princes of Armorican Brittany."[12] Completed in 1505 and surviving in only one manuscript, this work was later edited and published under the name of *Histoire de Bretagne*, by which it is usually known today.

Although Le Baud's output did not receive wide recognition at the time, it strongly influenced the much more successful account of his near contemporary Alain Bouchart, who enabled the Breton historiographical tradition to make the leap from manuscript to print. Bouchart was a notary and jurist who, as Duke François II's secretary, helped publish for the first time an edition of the fourteenth-century Breton customary laws (*Tres ancienne coutume de Bretagne*).[13] Although he, unlike Le Baud, originally opposed Duchess Anne's marriage to King Charles VIII, he changed his mind and quickly entered the upper echelons of royal service, spending the rest of his career in Paris. Anne's patronage allowed him to show the full potential of a national history of Brittany by giving the principality its own *Grandes croniques* analogous to those of France. The first, printed edition of 1514 survives in fourteen copies, and the first half of the sixteenth century saw four more editions (some extended by later anonymous authors), attesting the popularity of this narrative.[14]

The political context in which they wrote and the close relationship between their texts makes it possible to study Le Baud and Bouchart together as a pivotal stage in the historical narration of the Breton war of succession across the centuries. Looking forward, these two works essentially set the pattern for historians of Brittany up until the Revolution. First came Le Baud's great-nephew Bertrand d'Argentré (1519–1590), who likewise trained as a jurist and inherited Le Baud's materials. He was followed by the Benedictine historians of the Maurist school, who engaged in a number of sweeping projects covering different aspects of French and regional history.[15] Looking back, they built not only on the *Grandes chroniques de*

11 Le Baud, "'*Genealogie*,'" ed. Kerhervé, 522–24.

12 "Armorican" Brittany refers to the Breton peninsula, as opposed to the island of Great Britain.

13 Jones, "Bouchart, Alain."

14 Bouchart, *Grandes croniques*, ed. Auger et al., 1:7, 11.

15 Argentré, *Histoire de Bretaigne*; Lobineau, *Histoire de Bretagne*; Morice and Taillandier, *Histoire ecclésiastique et civile*.

France (which Le Baud preferred to refer to as the "book of deeds" of individual French kings), Froissart, and Cuvelier (either his original poem or the Prose Guesclin A), but also on the distinctive contributions of previous history-writers in the employ of the Montfort dukes. From the reign of Jean IV on, these writers were a mix of clerics and laymen, but they all held administrative positions in the ducal government that inspired their historical endeavours and gave them access to the records they needed to write them.[16] Naturally, these authors interested themselves in the Breton civil war. First, Guillaume de Saint-André wrote a moralizing poem in praise of his employer Jean IV after the duke's return to power in 1381. Completed by 1385 and surviving in four medieval manuscripts, this work used the duke's trials and tribulations to illustrate the vagaries of Fortune, though the later Montfortist writers appear to have been less interested in the poem's didactic aspect than in its content.[17] Next, the *Chronicon Briocense* or chronicle of Saint-Brieuc (so called for an invocation to that saint at the head of the manuscripts) was completed by 1416, in the reign of Jean V (r. 1399–1442). Its author was probably another of Jean IV's administrators, Hervé Le Grant, a ducal secretary and archivist who may have begun his work in the late years of that reign.[18] His was the first attempt to set Brittany into the wider course of world history, but his relatively dry, year-by-year account of events in Latin contrasts strikingly with the vivid, emotional rhymes of his colleague Saint-André. Although the *Chronicon* was again limited in popularity, with two surviving manuscripts of middling quality, Le Baud's notes copied many passages.[19] It was then under Duke François II that a concise, general history of the duchy was attempted in French, this time by his chamberlain Jean de Saint-Paul (ca. 1470), but this work now exists only in later fragments. The surviving portions concerning the war, from the 1350s onwards, largely followed Saint-André and Cuvelier.[20]

The memory of the Breton civil war within the more-or-less official ducal historiography thus occurred in three phases. Initially, writers personally acquainted with the triumphant Jean IV developed strongly parti-

16 Kerhervé, "Aux origines d'un sentiment national."

17 Saint-André, *Chronique*, ed. Cauneau and Philippe, 149.

18 Jones, *Le premier inventaire*, 69–86.

19 [Le Grant?], *Chronicon Briocense*, ed. Le Duc and Sterckx, 8. Since the part discussing the Breton civil war has only been edited as excerpts (Morice, ed., *Mémoires*, 1:42–57), I will instead cite from the text of the oldest manuscript, Paris, BnF, MS latin 6003.

20 Saint-Paul, *Chronique*, 3–47.

san works recounting the Montfortist version of events. Then, during the uncertainties of François II's rule and the precarious independence of the duchy under Anne, a revived interest in the arc of Breton history produced new syntheses that responded to present concerns while taking a more detached view of the civil war period. Finally, long after the duchy had been incorporated into the French domain, historians picked up on these later accounts to consolidate a narrative largely accepted until the later nineteenth century. Taking Le Baud and Bouchart as the culmination of the medieval narrative tradition and the jump-start of the early modern one is important for assessing their version of Jeanne's and Charles's joint reputations in three interconnected ways.

First, in comparison with the earlier authors, Le Baud and Bouchart were perhaps surprisingly balanced in their treatment of the civil war. These were partisan texts, rather than propagandic like those of Saint-André and Le Grant.[21] That is, they did not conceal all the messiness of the war as the foundations of the current dynasty even though they ultimately promoted its legitimacy. Le Baud even explicitly chose to follow Froissart's account because of its neutrality and attention to detail, and avoided using the ducal title on either side to forestall charges of favouritism.[22] Second, writing about these events from a distance of a century and a half, Le Baud and Bouchart generally relied on established accounts and on documentary evidence. Their originality therefore lay less in adding new material (though there are a few noteworthy exceptions), but in what they chose to retain or omit from previous authors and how they framed its significance. Third, for Le Baud and Bouchart, the civil war was only one part of the long sweep of Breton history, and from the Montfortist perspective Jeanne and Charles had never been the protagonists. Faced with evolving political concerns over the period of their writings, they did not make a concerted attempt to establish a single, definite picture of the Penthièvre duke and duchess. Instead, they dealt piecemeal with the different, even contradictory, legacies of their roles. Even as reputation moved from an ongoing dialogue to the authority (however complicated) of written tradition, then, it could always be contested. Nevertheless, a range of themes emerged, or were expanded upon, that spoke to the impact of gendered expectations and aristocratic partnership on reactions to the Breton civil war at the end of the independent duchy.

21 LBC, 14.

22 LBC, 315, 402.

An Unstable Partnership?

One way to criticize a ruler was to describe them with physical defects that supposedly reflected a wider moral failing. Although the idea that outward flaws reflected interior ones was by no means universally accepted in the Middle Ages, the potential link between disfigurement and sin could always be politically deployed.[23] In the case of kings, the metaphorical (or indeed, theological) link between the condition of their physical body and that of their realm meant that disability could be leveraged to their discredit.[24] While later medieval rulers were not generally disqualified purely on the basis of physical impairment, they remained unable to live up to the idealized princely body.[25] Ruling women were especially vulnerable to this type of attack, since in addition it also implied they fell short of specifically feminized body standards. A beautiful appearance was often considered a reflection of inner worth, making it an expected attribute of the nobility, and of women in particular.[26] But just as good queens were often represented as ideal beauties, so too could bad queens become ugly, deformed, even monstrous.[27]

These negative characterizations frequently developed long afterwards, and Jeanne's case is no exception. The chivalric chronicle tradition had sporadically mentioned Jeanne's feminine virtues. The few times she was described, Jeanne possessed the conventional assets of a lady, being called "a beautiful young girl" at her marriage in Froissart, while Cuvelier's Bertrand du Guesclin praised her goodness.[28] It was Bouchart who instead introduced the idea that Jeanne was lame (*boeteuse*), and even turned it into an epithet, Jeanne la Boiteuse.[29] Despite this late invention, it was taken as fact in the sixteenth century and persisted at least through the nineteenth.[30] Bouchart did not explain or comment further on the descrip-

23 Metzler, *Disability*, 46–47, 49, 51–54, 163.

24 Le Goff, "Mal royal," 106.

25 Lecuppre, "Déficience du corps."

26 Wilkinson, "Gendered Chivalry," 235.

27 E.g., Gibbons, "Isabeau of Bavaria," 55–56, 64–65; Huneycutt, "Creation of a Crone," 35; Turner, "Eleanor of Aquitaine," 20; Woodacre, "Leonor of Navarre," 168; Allirot, "*Male royne boiteuse*," 121; Green, "'A Woman Given to Slippery Ways'?," 317; Lewis, "Katherine of Valois," 126.

28 Rome, 462; Chanson, l. 1884.

29 GCB, 2:26, 33.

30 Graham-Goering, *Princely Power*, 36n1.

tion. Ironically, his patron Anne was lame herself; possibly, assigning this same characteristic to her predecessor was meant to redirect attention elsewhere, while restraining Bouchart's over-emphasis of this trait.

In itself, however, describing Jeanne as lame implied several things. Such lopsidedness could be associated with the Devil, and so signify an authority out of balance.[31] The most obvious referent here was Jeanne's legitimacy as duchess, which Bouchart thought was not legally grounded.[32] Her lameness visibly signalled the inadequate foundations of her title. For ruling women, there were also gendered considerations to lameness.[33] Jeanne's ability to physically carry out her duties as duchess were not hindered as a man's might have been since she was not expected to perform feats of arms.[34] However, a queen's crookedness could destabilize the "royal equilibrium" in two ways: either by exercising too much authority and so blurring the boundaries between queen and king, or by failing to adequately support her husband and guide him towards just rule.[35] In Jeanne's case, both might have applied, as she at once dominated Charles and corrupted his authority. Thus, either on her own or as part of a partnership, Jeanne's lameness subtly flagged her up as a misfit for her role.

The sudden introduction of this stereotypical critique in the late Montfortist tradition contrasts with an unexpectedly receptive attitude towards Charles's ongoing legacy as a virtuous prince or even a saint. Jean de Saint-Paul knew the Prose Guesclin B and paraphrased its eulogy for Charles by noting his chivalric glory (*honneur*) in seventeen (sic, a slight misreading of the original) of his eighteen battles.[36] While Le Baud's *Compillation* avoided such praise, his *Histoire* repeatedly commended Charles's knightly virtue.[37] Charles fought valiantly and vigorously at both La Roche-Derrien and Auray. He had been chosen as Jeanne's husband and champion by the Estates of Brittany (referring to a regional assembly of churchmen, nobility, and towns, which had not in fact existed before 1352), because even at

---

31 Ueltschi, *Pied qui cloche*, 192, 239, 244.

32 GCB, 2:43.

33 Cf. Ueltschi, *Pied qui cloche*, 278.

34 Jeanne's own succession case had cited lameness as a failing particularly for *male* heirs: Graham-Goering et al., *Aux origines de la guerre*, doc. 2, no. 87.

35 Bagerius and Ekholst, "For Better or for Worse," 640; Allirot, "*Male royne boiteuse*," 132; Parsons, "Queen's Intercession," 147; Jones, "Marguerite de Clisson," 349.

36 Saint-Paul, *Chronique*, 21.

37 LBH, 267, 304, 327, 329.

a young age he was a "prudent, wise, and virtuous prince." And after his death, Jean IV had him reverently and honourably buried "because he had been a good and worthy prince." Bouchart expanded this posthumous tribute, mentioning Charles's loyalty and that "his body was sanctified by the grace of God and they call him Saint Charles; and Pope Urban V approved and canonized him because he performed and still performs miracles every day."[38] Their acceptance of Charles's good character and even sanctity certainly reflected the decreased political threat it posed to the current ducal dynasty. However, it also opened space to play Charles and Jeanne off each other as good spouse/bad spouse, as Le Baud and Bouchart reopened the question of why the civil war failed to resolve sooner and more peaceably. By reusing and elaborating different aspects of the offshoot of the chivalric tradition discussed in Chapter 2, they created new readings of the lopsided responsibility for violence.

Back in the fourteenth century, Guillaume de Saint-André had been happy to make Charles entirely responsible for the diplomatic breakdown. For Charles, peacemaking was only a feint, not a commitment.[39] He did not care "a pennyworth" (*maillee*) for the peace accords proposed at Saint-Omer in 1361, and refused to match Jean IV's show of goodwill negotiation at the Landes d'Évran in 1363.[40] Worse still, when Jean gave Charles another chance to fulfill these broken promises before Auray, Charles remained hard-hearted, unwilling to settle for less than the whole of Brittany even though it belonged rightfully to Jean.[41] Meanwhile, Saint-André minimized Jeanne's authority, mentioning her only twice in the whole poem.[42] After all, since he was writing within a decade of Charles's near-canonization and before the release of Jeanne's son Jean from captivity, Charles's reputation likely seemed the greater threat to Montfort legitimacy, though this version still appealed much later to Jean de Saint-Paul.[43]

Charles's diplomatic duplicity fed into a sustained attack on his wartime conduct in this work. As part of his moralizing aims, Saint-André played up the contrasts between Jean IV and Charles according to mascu-

---

38 GCB, 2:92.

39 Saint-André, *Chronique*, ll. 665–69.

40 Saint-André, *Chronique*, ll. 551–52, 891–980.

41 Saint-André, *Chronique*, ll. 1174–77.

42 Saint-André, *Chronique*, ll. 604, 1505.

43 Saint-Paul, *Chronique*, 16–17.

linized standards of justice, piety, and chivalry. He reiterated Jean's pursuit of a righteous, divinely sanctioned war while stressing that Charles had no lawful claim to the ducal title.[44] This false authority undermined Charles not only as a prince but as a knight, fighting under an insignia to which he was not entitled.[45] Indeed, Charles's behaviour was hardly chivalrous either on or off the battlefield. A trucebreaker, he revealed an inappropriate bloodthirstiness by swearing to kill not only Jean, but anyone captured alive at Auray, a breach of the usual (if complicated) norms of war and an echo of the cruelty that had challenged witnesses at the canonization.[46] It was Jean rather than Charles who called for the battle to be postponed to respect the feast day of Saint Michael, as the Church asked of knights, but the offer was rejected.[47] At several encounters, Charles's knights were willing to fight only with superior numbers or not even then, a cowardice that reflected badly on Charles's leadership.[48] And where Jean responded gently to insults, Charles was bitter with vengeance and scorned courtesy.[49] The humility and courtliness that had formerly contributed to Charles's positive reputation were here reassigned. Worse even was the fact that Charles was an oath-breaker. Whereas Jean took his pledges as seriously as the Mass, Charles took no care of his own, and his faithlessness was a recurring theme.[50] This perfidy violated the "trueness" at the heart of the construction of knightly manhood.[51] In this light, Charles's failure to bring about peace was a masculine rather than a feminine problem.

Subsequent Montfortist writers, however, increasingly brought Jeanne into the picture. The *Chronicon Briocense*, which also repeated the tale of Charles's brutality at Quimper from the anonymous *Chronicon Britannicum*, portrayed him as unwilling to fulfill his promises from Évran, a lapse that led more or less directly to his death at Auray.[52] This fate, Le Grant noted, "was nothing to wonder at since Charles went against his oaths

44 Saint-André, *Chronique*, ll. 446, 1246–54, 1290–94, 1301; 505, 509–16, 799.

45 Saint-André, *Chronique*, ll. 1271–74.

46 Saint-André, *Chronique*, ll. 833–34, 1193–200; Ambühl, *Prisoners of War*, chap. 1.

47 Saint-André, *Chronique*, ll. 1201–30.

48 Saint-André, *Chronique*, ll. 657, 692–700, 790–95, 887–90.

49 Saint-André, *Chronique*, ll. 459, 464, 831–32, 1015–17.

50 Saint-André, *Chronique*, ll. 655, 744, 834–35, 1189–92.

51 McVitty, "False Knights," 459–60.

52 BnF, MS lat. 6003, fol. 102v.

made upon the body of the Lord and the holy Gospels of God."[53] However, he added, rumour had it that this lamentable volte-face was provoked by his wife and his other counsellors.[54] By suggesting that Charles was being led rather than leading, the question of fault became more ambiguous.

Le Baud intensified Jeanne's responsibility, saying she disrupted the peace talks not only at the Landes d'Évran, but also on two occasions prior to Auray. At each point, his two versions nuanced the exact dynamics implied. At Évran, the *Compillation* claimed it was "milady the wife of milord Charles" herself who broke the treaty, because she did not wish to cede Nantes or the other towns specified therein.[55] Charles accommodated her because he depended on her for his right to the duchy. The agency given to Jeanne in light of her inheritance here showcased the dangers of female succession. Le Baud's *Histoire* instead took a step back and again identified Jeanne (here referred to as the countess of Penthièvre and Lord Charles's wife) as foremost among the counsellors who instigated his contravention of the accords.[56] At the same time, Le Baud escalated Charles's desire to merely please (*complaire*) his wife, which now became a more thorough obedience or submission (*obtemperer*). Charles's subordination undercut his ability to demonstrate a manly control. Yet, Le Baud now conceded, it was out of character for Charles to break his word, "for he is attested to have been a good prince, true and loyal." By redeeming Charles's trueness and showing Jeanne as the one acting out of place, the abortive peace became once more a failure of femininity, but also downplayed Jeanne's status as heiress.

The dealings before Auray likewise developed Jeanne's culpability to differing degrees. The *Compillation* reported that Charles notified his wife of the eleventh-hour compromise directly, in recognition that the ducal title lay with her.[57] She refused it, and persuaded him to do likewise, giving her a lead role but ultimately making them jointly responsible. The *Histoire* attributed Jeanne's refusal to her strong mettle, and Charles simply reported her decision back to the count of Montfort.[58] In the lead-up to these events,

---

53 BnF, MS lat. 6003, fol. 103r, "Nec est mirandum ex hoc quia idem Karolus contra juramentum suum supra corpus domini et sancta dei evangelia per ipsum factum et prestitum."

54 "Uxore sua et aliis suis consiliariis ut dicebatur instigantibus."

55 LBC, 384.

56 LBH, 321.

57 LBC, 388.

58 LBH, 324.

Le Baud reported Charles's leave-taking from Jeanne, including her speech extracting his promise to give away no part of the duchy.[59] His earlier version matched Froissart's nearly word-for word. In the second, Jeanne no longer called upon God to witness her rightful title, only the Breton barons in attendance, slightly tempering her claim. Much more importantly, Le Baud added that Charles "was most gentle and courteous" and would have gladly agreed to peace, if he had not been so urged (*sollicité*) by his wife and knights. The cumulative effect of these scenes was ambivalent, as the straightforward reporting of Jeanne's justifications could even verge upon the positive. Yet her high-handedness and rigidity were increasingly problematized, while Charles's primary fault was reduced to an inability to resist his wife.

The story finally presented by Bouchart did away with these nuances. Having efficiently skipped straight over the Landes d'Évran, he made Jeanne solely responsible for brow-beating Charles before Auray.[60] This time, Jeanne having said her piece, Charles departed for battle, whereupon his knights and squires took pains to console him. In addition to being gentle and courteous, Charles was now described as being *humain*—kindly, benevolent, or compassionate. Unfortunately, Bouchart concluded, "he was so put upon by his wife" that he could not go back, "because of which great harm befell him thereafter." The knights had shifted to Charles's side, leaving Jeanne alone to ruin her husband. Jeanne's aggressive domineering, whose possible sexual connotations (cf. Chapter 2) may have become even clearer with the knights out of the picture, almost physically reversed the expected gender of command.

These reinterpretations provide a rich opportunity to understand how the circulation of information interacted with the choices of individual chroniclers. Transmitting reputation across a patchwork of textual authorities was an iterative process. As I showed in Chapter 2, Jeanne's failure as a peacemaker initially evolved circuitously across different branches of the Froissart and Cuvelier narratives. Since Saint-André wrote around the same time as Cuvelier, Jeanne's role in rejecting compromise had scarcely entered the discourse, and he consistently condemned Charles. By Le Grant's time, Cuvelier's version of events must have become known from either his poem or the Prose Guesclin A, although Le Grant simplified the chronology by conflating the Auray and Évran negations, and made Jeanne the ringleader of the ill-advisors, rather than the more indirect association in Cuvelier. The

59 LBC, 386–87; LBH, 323–24.

60 GCB, 2:84.

options expanded in the late fifteenth and early sixteenth centuries. Le Baud followed Le Grant's positioning of this episode, but evidently also encountered multiple copies of both the Guesclin and Froissart stories. His *Compillation* used Froissart's original version of the leave-taking scene, but he later switched to one of the variant manuscripts blaming Jeanne. This change may reflect access to new material following Anne's elevation to queen of France. Bouchart probably saw that manuscript too, since he reverted to the original vocabulary which Le Baud had modified. More surprisingly, in addition to the standard version of Cuvelier, Le Baud used the Prose Guesclin B for Jeanne's reaction to the negotiations at Auray. The pro-Penthièvre sympathies of this work were not reflected in his *Compillation* but made it into his *Histoire*'s description of Jeanne as highly spirited, a trait whose positive connotations he let stand.[61] Likewise, Le Baud used Saint-André to critique Charles's trustworthiness over previous truces, but rejected the poet's interpretation of the Landes d'Évran and contrasted Charles's personal chivalry with his troops' despair.[62] The fluidity with which these authors approached their sources meant that rewrites were sometimes more conservative while elsewhere they innovated—which explains the difficulties historians often encounter in trying to date chronicle versions based on originality.

The non-linear development of Jeanne's and Charles's reputations for warmongering demonstrates the particular malleability of gendered critiques in the context of shared power. Both masculinity and femininity could be violated through the failure to make peace (or indeed wage war) correctly, but the emphasis depended on the sliding scale between individual and joint responsibility, as well as different hierarchies within the latter. The late Montfortist chroniclers helped themselves freely across the range of options, cherry-picking and juxtaposing pieces of information without trying to reconcile them. Under the pressure of multiple viable norms, then, reputations had a tendency to fragment. The personas of Jeanne and Charles continued to feed back on each other, but the effect was more kaleidoscopic than harmonic.

---

61 His restraint contrasted with the expanded version of this scene in Argentré, *Histoire de Bretaigne*, 473: "The said de Blois let his wife know what had happened, and sent her the signed terms to see. This lady was no coward, and she immediately picked up the scent and got angry; and she said it straight, that the said de Blois her husband, was selling too cheaply that which did not belong to him." By turning Jeanne into an angry scold, this treatment effectively turned praise into a caricature of an uppity woman.

62 LBC, 381, 383; LBH, 319.

An Integrated Partnership?

Perhaps the easiest way to criticize a woman in a position of power was to go after her feminine qualities and portray her as a failed mother and/or wife. Domineering queens were said to abandon their children or even cause their deaths, or conversely, to nurture children born out of wedlock as if the king's own.[63] Certain queen mothers were also condemned for refusing to cede power to their offspring, abusing their maternal authority to rule in their stead.[64] Jeanne, however, was largely spared posthumous comments on her shortcomings as a mother or spouse. Despite Charles's long absence in England, she was never accused of infidelity, a strategy we might expect from hostile chroniclers to discredit her descendants and undermine their claim to the ducal title. Because the late Montfortist writers were primarily concerned with patriotic questions of dynasty, however, Jeanne's claim as heiress meant confronting the relative roles of men and women within the ducal lineage, and deciding who did and did not belong in the Breton family. Their interpretation of both Jeanne's and Charles's familial relationships was therefore complicated and unsettled.

For Le Baud and Bouchart, the issue of female succession underpinning the war was intimately bound up with the political circumstances in which they wrote each version of events. From a legal perspective, they became progressively less antagonistic to excluding women as heirs while (of course) maintaining that Jeanne's particular claim was invalid. They did so by nuancing their evaluations of the formal judgement by the French *parlement* that had originally granted the duchy to Charles on Jeanne's behalf.

At first, Le Baud opposed female succession through a detailed rebuttal of the sentence of Conflans given in favour of the Penthièvre suit.[65] Women, he argued, could not inherit a kingdom, and so likewise could not claim the duchy of Brittany, which had its own royal past.[66] He also asserted that male heirs had always taken precedence over female ones in Brittany. Both these

63 Vallée-Karcher, "Jeanne de Bourgogne," 96; Allirot, "*Male royne boiteuse*," 122–24; Gibbons, "Isabeau of Bavaria," 57–59, 67–71; Adams, *Life and Afterlife*, 40–47; Turner, "Eleanor of Aquitaine," 26, 29; Green, "'A Woman Given to Slippery Ways'?," 318.

64 Huneycutt, "Creation of a Crone," 35; McCannon, "Two Queens," 163–64; cf. Turner, "Eleanor of Aquitaine," 37; Benz, "Conspiracy and Alienation," 120; Lewis, "Katherine of Valois," 129, 132–37.

65 LBC, 311–12.

66 Women's inability to succeed to the French throne had developed in legal theory over the fourteenth and fifteenth centuries: Taylor, "Salic Law."

arguments had been summarized in the *Songe du vergier*, a political treatise produced in the 1370s to prove, among other things, Charles V's right to confiscate Brittany from Jean IV, but which later appealed for its selective summaries of the original succession debate.[67] Le Baud's exclusion of women as heirs legitimized the Montfort dynasty at a moment of weakness, for their successions had not passed smoothly from father to son since 1450. In the early 1470s, Jean II, the powerful lord of Rohan (1452–1516), asserted the rights of his wife Marie de Bretagne (1446–1511) as legitimate heiress of the duchy according to the rules of succession prior to the treaty of Guérande.[68] Although his ambitions were more vaguely defined, Le Baud's first patron Jean de Derval positioned himself as part of the ducal family and likely aspired to follow the then-childless Duke François.[69] Reaffirming the dynasty's commitment to masculine inheritance was therefore pressing.

By contrast, Le Baud later squarely foregrounded the possibility of female succession. His *Genealogie* acknowledged the novelty of the Montfortist position on the exclusion of female heirs, and noted that the count had seized and occupied the duchy. Jean Kerhervé has argued that this work aimed to show that the heir's gender mattered less than the prestige of the dynasty.[70] However, handling this transitional moment actually meant promoting different gendered roles, because it was easier to justify one unsuccessful female inheritance when women did not personally perform the ducal role. Throughout this work, Le Baud focused on the men who had come to power through their wives or mothers, not the Breton countesses and duchesses themselves. This approach reflected the new political circumstances facing the duchy in 1486. After Anne's birth in 1477, Jean de Rohan had switched tactics to advance his own claims according to a masculine line of succession, a title he would reassert in 1492 after the death of François II.[71] It was therefore useful for Le Baud to reopen the possibility of female inheritance to secure the position of his patron's daughter and preclude rivals, while acknowledging the important role that the nine-year-old Anne's eventual husband would inevitably play.

---

67 [Le Fèvre?], *Songe du vergier*, 1:260.

68 Gicquel, "Jean II de Rohan," 5.

69 Mauger, *Aristocratie et mécénat*, 32–33.

70 Le Baud, "'*Genealogie*,'" ed. Kerhervé, 521.

71 Gicquel, "Jean II de Rohan," 6, 8.

Le Baud finally developed a third interpretation in his *Histoire*.[72] In his critique of Conflans, he avoided the issue of gendered succession entirely, preferring to summarize a few points relating to the mechanics of succession drawn from Froissart and the *Grandes chroniques*. He directed his readers to the *Songe* for further information, but refrained from wading deeper into the debate himself. After all, writing for Duchess Anne in her prime of life, he had no wish to undercut her authority. In contrast with her first marriage, Anne was able to exert herself on a much more even footing with her second husband. Meanwhile, the threat of the Penthièvre claim had finally been put to rest for good. Jeanne's great-granddaughter and last remaining heiress, Nicole de Bretagne, had sold her rights to Brittany to King Louis XI (r. 1461–1483) for 50,000 *livres* in 1480. A beautiful family tree made in the early 1490s, probably to celebrate Anne's marriage to King Charles VIII, showed a happy resolution to the civil war through the union of the respective heirs of Jean and Jeanne.[73] Since Anne's marriage with her second husband, Louis XII, had only consolidated her position as ruler of her duchy, there was more leeway to tolerate Jeanne near the top of the princely hierarchy.

Just before Anne's death and the succession of her daughter Claude, Bouchart reduced female inheritance to a non-issue. Rather than debating any points of law, he simply translated the text of the sentence of Conflans, including the Montfortist points against female heirs but also those of Jeanne and Charles in favour.[74] He then reported that Jean de Montfort was not surprised at the outcome because he had anticipated Philippe's favouritism towards his nephew. This framing suggested that the case was less a precedent than a fluke.[75] Also, unlike Le Baud, Bouchart did not warn of the risks of female succession when reporting Jean III's earlier attempt to trade Brittany to the king of France. This story, adapted from a fourteenth-century Parisian chronicle, had originally given Jeanne some agency as the niece "who said she had the right to the duchy."[76] However, a woman inheriting such an important territory was considered a threat to the kingdom at large, a premise which Le Baud accepted in both major versions of his

72 LBH, 274.

73 Nantes, Archives départementales de Loire-Atlantique, E 6-4. My thanks to Michael Jones for drawing my attention to the document's production context.

74 GCB, 2:39–43.

75 Cf. GCB, 2:93.

76 Géraud, ed., *Chronique latine de Guillaume de Nangis*, 2:144.

narrative.[77] For Bouchart, the risk was only that Jean de Montfort would not tolerate Jeanne as duchess.[78] Because his chronicle did not contest the principle of female succession at any point, the legal issue gave ground to personal perspectives and ambitions.

This clear progression in the legal interpretation of women's place in the ducal dynasty contrasted with a more complicated portrayal of the social implications. Viewing the succession in masculine terms reflected patrilineal norms that expected noble families to transmit their legacies via a series of male heirs. However, it was common enough to run out of sons that alternatives were regularly sought.[79] One solution lay in the fact that a majority of noblewomen ended up marrying into families of lower status than their own.[80] This power imbalance meant that sometimes a husband agreed to join his wife's family instead of vice versa, giving them a male representative to whom they could pass on their identity and authority. Focusing on Charles's authority rather than Jeanne's therefore entailed defining his place within the Breton ducal lineage, whereas allowing for female succession made this belonging more negotiable.

This dynamic is apparent in comparing Le Baud's first and last versions of how Jean III attempted to arrange his own succession.[81] In the *Compilation*, Le Baud claimed that the duke chose Charles as Jeanne's husband thinking that Charles should succeed him, with Jeanne's own claim coming only as an afterthought. He noted (probably following the *Songe du vergier*) that the marriage arrangements specified that Charles and his heirs would bear the name and coat-of-arms of Brittany.[82] These symbols represented not just the ducal authority but the act of joining their kindred.[83] This report created a line of male succession, having Charles take Jeanne's place in the family. It was Charles's position as heir which Le Baud criticized for impinging on Jean de Montfort's rights, and he reported with some satisfaction that nearly all the barons who swore to follow Charles had been killed in battle.[84] In his *Histoire*, however, he repeatedly stressed that Jean III thought

77 LBC, 300; LBH, 266.

78 GCB, 2:33.

79 Nassiet, "Parenté et successions dynastiques," 621.

80 Nassiet, *Parenté*, 137, 140–42.

81 LBC, 300–301; LBH, 267–68.

82 [Le Fèvre?], *Songe du vergier*, 1:261–62.

83 Cf. Nassiet, "Parenté et successions dynastiques," 622–23.

84 This observation sits a little oddly in a work dedicated to Jean de Derval, whose

Jeanne should succeed him and possess (*avoir*) the duchy after his death. Charles was then selected to defend Jeanne's right and to handle (*traicter*) the duchy. The verbs chosen for each spouse presented Charles as working on his wife's behalf, more a manager than a duke in his own right. Le Baud later reported that "according to certain authors" Charles could have succeeded to the duchy himself if he had assumed the familial identity of the Breton dukes, but he did not endorse this interpretation, and added that these unnamed authors said Duke Jean had forced the barons to perform homage to Charles. When Jeanne's rights were taken more seriously, Charles was only able to access the ducal authority by proxy, and his status within the family was called into doubt.

In fact, Le Baud and Bouchart were generally much more willing to incorporate Jeanne into their understanding of the ducal lineage than they were Charles, in keeping with the ongoing significance of powerful matrilineal connections within the French nobility at large.[85] Charles's identity as part of the Breton line was never secure among the chroniclers. Froissart and Cuvelier (and even the Prose Guesclin B) already consistently referred to him as Charles "de Blois," rather then "de Bretagne," a practice continued by Le Baud and Bouchart despite the story about him adopting the Breton name, arms, and battle-cry. They also went further in developing Charles's own familial identity. For Froissart, Charles's royal affiliation had been an important attribute, and it remained so here, but the Montfortists also focused on defining Charles's affiliation with the counts of Blois. This point of his identity had confused some copyists of Froissart's A text, who mistook Charles to *be* the count of Blois (an error that periodically crops up even in modern scholarship).[86] After discussing the marriage arrangements, Bouchart insisted that "you should know that the counts of Blois, for their surname, did not have the name of Blois, but they had the name of Châtillon. And so, to speak truly, this Charles should have the name of Châtillon, as I have read it in chronicles of the period."[87] Le Baud claimed that Charles's taking the Breton arms had been conditional upon his renunciation of "his name of Châtillon or of Blois," though he also acknowledged a tenuous connection to Brittany via Jean III's first wife and Charles's mother, who were

---

own ancestors fell solidly into that category.

85 Chassel, "Nom et les armes"; cf. Duindam, "Gender, Succession and Dynastic Rule."

86 Oxford, Bodleian Library, Laud misc. 745, fol. 34r; Paris, BnF, MS français 2647, fol. 73r, and MS français 2677, fol. 69v.

87 GCB, 2:34.

sisters.[88] The sensitivity of the choice of surname was likewise illustrated by Le Baud's insistence that French references to Jean IV as "de Montfort" did not stop the Bretons from recognizing him as "of the direct generation of their ancient princes."[89] These authors used familial affiliation to argue for inclusion or exclusion in the schematic understanding of the lines of power.

The treatment of Charles contrasts with how Le Baud and Bouchart insisted on Jeanne's affiliation with her natal family, in a way absent from the earlier tradition. The distinction was communicated through surnames, as when Le Baud spoke of "Jeanne de Bretagne, daughter [of Guy] and Charles de Blois, her husband," and Bouchart of "milord Charles de Blois and milady Jeanne de Bretagne his wife."[90] Jeanne regularly had her full name from the *Genealogie* onwards, so that no matter which spouse was taken as the starting point, their family lines could be kept separate. These cues were markers of legitimacy and standing within the family. Similarly, when Olivier de Clisson began to look for suitable marriage partners for his daughters in the mid-1380s, he thought of Jeanne and Charles's eldest son Jean, count of Penthièvre.[91] Jean, Olivier reflected, was of august extraction from both France (because his paternal grandmother had been the king's sister) and Brittany (because his mother—that is, Jeanne—was the daughter of Duke Arthur's younger son). While Le Baud identified Jeanne only via a junior member of the Breton family, it was emphatically her rather than Charles who brought in this link at all. The convention of referring to Jeanne as "de Penthièvre," which persists on the merits of better distinguishing her from many other Jeannes, dates (as far as I can trace) only to the eighteenth century and implied that she was part not of the main ducal family but of its second noble house.[92] Le Baud and Bouchart preferred to stress Jeanne's membership within the dynasty they served.

There was thus no real need to impugn Jeanne's marital reputation, as happened to other women. Jeanne's relative security within the late Montfortist conception of the ducal dynasty meant that it was Charles, not her, who represented a convenient weak link in the claims of their descendants. Attacking Jeanne would only have reflected badly on her dynasty, and it was possible to distance her heirs from the ducal title by other means. Jeanne

88 LBH, 267–68.

89 LBH, 319.

90 LBH, 270; GCB, 2:84.

91 LBC, 454.

92 Lobineau, *Histoire de Bretagne*, 2:308, for the first instance.

and Charles had five children who featured in the Montfortist chronicles. Their affiliation to either parent, however, was inconsistent. Le Baud's *Histoire* particularly insisted on Charles's role as a progenitor, mentioning on three separate occasions the children that Charles had produced from Jeanne.[93] Previously, it was Jeanne who had gotten children by Charles.[94] By foregrounding one parent over the other, these writers were able to reconfigure the ducal family tree as they saw fit.

This pattern is again most visible with their eldest son (whose date of birth Le Baud remarkably happened to note).[95] Jean's self-styling as "de Bretagne" raised some thorny issues. Unsurprisingly, his use of the ducal name and arms met with disapproval in the Montfortist chronicles. Le Baud reported Jean IV's sarcastic reaction to his cousin's presumption: "We are willing that he call himself Jean, for it is his proper name, and count of Penthièvre, but we wish him to set aside the [ducal] ermines and write 'Jean de Blois' or 'de Châtillon', and bear the arms of Châtillon and no others."[96] This demand forcefully prioritized Jean's patrilineal identity at the expense of his matrilineal connections. Nevertheless, Le Baud eventually conceded that Jean might want to retain some affiliation with the Breton family to which his mother's origins entitled him, in which case he could modify the Châtillon arms with a modest use of ermines.[97] However, Le Baud still intended to exclude Jean from the Breton ducal lineage, as comparison with his contemporaries shows. Bouchart, discussing the treaty of Guérande, instead noted Jeanne's ongoing right to use the full arms of Brittany, while her children would only need to modify these by adding a red border.[98] He even asserted that Jeanne's own heirs, female as well as male, were potential claimants to the ducal title, and referred to Jean as "de Bretagne" without further comment.[99] Saint-Paul before him had similarly reported that Jeanne retained the lifetime title of duchess of Brittany.[100] The actual treaty had made no such concessions, instead reserving the name and arms to Jean IV.[101] These revi-

93 LBH, 311–12, 320, 330.

94 LBG, 555.

95 LBH, 296.

96 LBC, 457; cf. LBH, 402–3, 406, 409, 410.

97 LBH, 410.

98 GCB, 2:95.

99 GCB, 2:96, 148–49. Cf. LBH, 333, 381, 391, who preferred "de Blois."

100 Saint-Paul, *Chronique*, 24.

101 Morice, ed., *Mémoires*, 1:1590.

sions showed a more inclusive attitude towards Jeanne and her posterity as part of the Breton dynasty, where Le Baud had preferred to see the counts of Penthièvre branching off or even transferring dynasties completely. If a patrilineal dynastic model remained the default, emphasizing matrilineal ties remained a viable means of constructing continuity or discontinuity to suit immediate interests.

The paramount importance of constructing the idealized ducal dynasty meant that Le Baud and Bouchart not only assessed Jeanne and Charles as claimants to a title, but measured them against the gendered roles of parenting. Charles bore the greatest blame for threatening familial interests by not fulfilling his responsibilities as a father. Importantly, this disruption did not stem from Charles's alleged extramarital affairs, which received at least passing attention. Froissart had reported that Charles's bastard son "Jean" died alongside him at Auray, and Le Baud and Bouchart embraced this detail.[102] Such evidence of adultery would not have carried the same stigma for a nobleman as for a noblewoman, and by the fifteenth century bastard children had come to play an important and publicly recognized role in furthering paternal political ambitions and familial strategies among the upper aristocracy.[103] Moreover, this rumour—which scandalized François Plaine, the modern advocate of Charles's sanctity—shows how Charles's reputation for strict chastity in 1371 did not appeal as strongly to secular historiographers.[104] Although the Church and the law morally disapproved of illicit sex, romantic chivalric ideals could instead see the resulting offspring as the outcome of knightly service to ladies, and so a fulfillment of noble manhood.[105]

Rather, problems arose with how Charles used his sons Jean and Guy as hostages for his ransom. According to Le Baud, Charles left them in England so that he could be released to secure the required sum, while Bouchart thought they had actually been captured alongside Charles at La Roche-Derrien.[106] As Rémy Ambühl has shown, a captured knight's children made for "ideal" hostages because "fatherly love and the concern for the perpetuation of a lineage" could be expected to encourage the knight's prompt payment

102 Amiens, 3:348; FrB, 6:168; LBC, 395, 397; LBH, 328; GCB, 2:89–90.

103 Karras and Pierpont, *Sexuality in Medieval Europe*, 189; Harsgor, "Essor des bâtards," 327, 331–33.

104 Plaine, "De l'autorité de Froissard," 21; but cf. Lewis, *Kingship and Masculinity*, 130, 257.

105 Harsgor, "Essor des bâtards," 350.

106 LBC, 371; LBH, 311; GCB, 2:70.

and good behaviour.[107] Normally, then, this exchange would not have raised any eyebrows. Charles, however, turned his thoughts towards revenge upon his release on parole, which led him to pursue an ill-advised strategy.[108] Rather than raising funds through the expected channels of his dependents and his French allies, he proceeded to make war on the countess of Montfort. Though technically allowed within the terms of his ransom as he did not fight in person, this plan resulted in the disastrous battle of Mauron in which Charles's much larger force was wiped out, a thorough defeat that spoke for itself. While in Le Baud's *Histoire* it appears that Charles simply forgot about his children in his desire to strike back against his foes, the *Compillation* explicitly made Charles's objective in this campaign to "conquer something which would profit him to get back his two sons."[109] But his failure in this risky approach left his sons imprisoned. Nor could Charles save any face for himself in the process, since his inability to arm himself kept him at home with his wife, undercutting his chivalric manliness.

Charles's initial misstep was compounded by the long-term implications of the situation. The Montfortist chroniclers agreed that had the kings of France and England wished to find a solution to the Breton war, Charles would have recovered his children from their imprisonment (and prolonged his own lifespan).[110] While this breakdown of peace negotiations was not Charles's fault, it was he—and, noticeably, not Jeanne—who bore the consequences as the one responsible for their captivity in the first place. The subsequent length of Jean and Guy's imprisonment and the toll it took on them (especially Guy, who died in England) became a recurring theme, always with the reminder that it was on their father's behalf or by his doing that they were there.[111] After Charles's death, moreover, "there was no one left from his side to take up the war nor the rights which he claimed, because Jean and Guy, his two oldest sons, to whom the matter related and belonged, were prisoners in England."[112] Le Baud transferred the weight of defeat to Charles and his children, cutting Jeanne out of the picture (despite having acknowledged just a few lines earlier that it was to her that Jean III had given the duchy). Charles's inability to redeem his sons from captivity imperilled

107 Ambühl, *Prisoners of War*, 252.

108 LBC, 371; LBH, 311.

109 LBC, 372.

110 LBC, 380; LBH, 318; GCB, 2:79.

111 LBC, 448, 454–55; LBH, 330, 381, 391.

112 LBC, 399; cf. LBH, 331.

his lineage and its interests, as well as straining the bonds of affection that should have united father and sons.

Jeanne's maternal role was, on the whole, relatively understated. Froissart, as we saw, had emphasized Jeanne's affective motherhood at specific points in his narrative. In his Rome version, Jeanne used her young sons Jean and Guy to help her rally support after Charles's capture.[113] Amiens and the Abridgement showed the widowed duchess mourning the imprisonment of her two eldest sons and (in Amiens alone) taking comfort in her remaining son, young Henri.[114] Louis d'Anjou was especially willing to support Jeanne because he had married her daughter, making Jeanne his mother too.[115] These versions were not in wide circulation, so few of these anecdotes were later adopted. Conversely, small details introduced by the late Montfortists painted a more negative picture. Bouchart reconfigured Louis's relationship as Charles's son-in-law rather than Jeanne's, even though she was the focus of this interaction.[116] Le Baud outlined a parallel between the two parents, who were unable to retain their children. After Auray, one of Charles's sons was in Nantes with his mother, but was given into his sister's care out of fear of Jean IV; thus, of their three sons, the two eldest were held in an English prison for their father, and the third was sent away by his mother to France.[117] Jeanne's forced separation from her child also mirrored that of Jeanne de Flandre, giving the Montfortists a sort of poetic justice. Later, Jeanne's death meant that Jean despaired of ever being rescued from prison; if his father had put him there, his mother had been his last hope.[118]

But Jeanne was able to make up for this scattering of her family in a way that Charles never was, because she signed the treaty of Guérande with the victorious duke and so gave her descendants significant rights. Le Baud and Bouchart consistently recognized that should Jean IV have died without sons, Jeanne's heirs (or those of herself and Charles) would have been entitled to reclaim the duchy of Brittany.[119] It was also Jeanne alone who was to enjoy the county of Penthièvre, and pass it on in turn to her eldest son.[120]

113 Rome, 818.

114 Amiens, 3:356; Abridged, 418.

115 Cf. FrB, 6:173.

116 GCB, 2:92.

117 LBH, 330.

118 LBC, 455; LBH, 391.

119 LBC, 401–2; LBH, 333; GCB, 2:96.

120 LBC, 473–74; LBH, 410; GCB, 2:95.

By securing her children's future, she fulfilled a core responsibility of motherhood. Nor did this provision have to come at the expense of Jeanne's personal interests. The lands were hers, and thereafter her son's: this was one point where Jeanne's place in the succession was not contested. The fact that Jean was imprisoned until after her death may have influenced this narrative, as he was unable to administer the lands in any case, so she could not reasonably be expected to hand them over. Nevertheless, the net result was that Jeanne's ongoing authority as countess of Penthièvre preserved her son's rights rather than usurping them, compensating for Charles's lapse and maintaining an honourable position within the Breton ducal family.

An Alternative Partnership?

As a result of the late Montfortists' dynastic readings, Jeanne's prominence in the narrative of the civil war had tended to increase, impacting her reputation for leadership for better or worse. She was often mentioned at Charles's side where she had not been in Froissart, and was shown at the head of her party more regularly.[121] Yet despite the importance of this partnership, these chronicles also developed her solo career after her husband's death in new ways. The prolonged coda of the war—or indeed, its constant crisis—meant that her authority in this period could be reimagined outside the context of her earlier collaboration. The political reconfiguration during the rebellion of 1379–1380 meant that Jeanne's primary counterpart became instead Duke Jean IV, her former rival. She kept her familiar position at the head of the Breton barons, but her status as countess of Penthièvre rather than duchess of Brittany meant that she could contribute to Montfortist interests in a new way.

Froissart's B text was the first to include Jeanne among the partisans of the duke-in-exile. He noted that several knights and squires took part in this alliance, as well as "the countess of Penthièvre, mother of the children of Brittany."[122] She was notably the only supporter so specifically identified, though Froissart did not give her an explicit leadership role here. Indeed, her status was ambivalent: countess, she nevertheless remained a link in the legitimate ducal line. The implication could be that her participation was meant to preserve the interests of her children in the duchy as a whole, as specified in the treaty of Guérande.

---

121 LBH, e.g., 319; GCB, e.g., 2:43, 44, 49, 70.

122 FrB, 9:137.

The complexity of this situation, however, may have prompted Froissart to revisit her motivations in the C version of the text.[123] Here, among other new details, he stressed the opposition to the royal takeover across gendered lines: not only lords, barons, and knights, but also ladies and damsels, collectively called for government according to Breton laws. Froissart found it remarkable that the countess of Penthièvre herself agreed with them.[124] This time, though, he linked her engagement not to the ducal title, but to protecting the liberties of her lands and subjects. Her position as countess streamlined her cooperation with the duke compared to framing her as a rival. These independent interests also augmented Jeanne's authority, although Froissart still did not specify how exactly she contributed to the rebellion.

That angle came instead from the Montfortist historiographical tradition. Saint-André, as usual, skipped over Jeanne entirely, perhaps because he was particularly aware that Jeanne had opposed the king more than she had supported Jean during these quite recent events. But Le Grant developed Jeanne into the ringleader of the Breton rebels who rallied behind Jean. Her agency first operated in the legal sphere.[125] With Jean IV unable to respond to a court summons of which he was unaware, it was Jeanne who fought the royal sentence of confiscation. She ordered several prominent and learned Bretons from among her servitors to argue that the king was unlawfully attempting to deprive the duke of his rights. Moreover, even supposing that such a confiscation was licit, he could not then prejudice the rights of Jeanne herself and of her children based on the terms of Guérande. Le Grant presumably felt justified in reporting this display of unexpected altruism, where Jeanne placed the duke's needs above her own, based on the logic of the *Songe du vergier*. This text tackled Jean IV's expected claims first, followed by Jeanne's.[126] By lumping them together as the case put forward by Jeanne's representatives, however, Le Grant neatly acknowledged the potential divergence of her interests while still moving her into the Montfortist camp. Similarly, he referred to her as both countess of Penthièvre and the duke's first cousin. This designation legitimized her as part of the wider

123 Chicago, Newberry Library, MS Case f.37.2, fol. 77r.

124 The word he used, *proprement*, could have stressed either Jeanne's personal involvement as a high-profile player, the veracity of this report clarifying her participation, or the significance of her rallying to the Montfort camp.

125 BnF, MS lat. 6003, fol. 106v.

126 [Le Fèvre?], *Songe du vergier*, 1:258–63.

ducal family but, by foregrounding her separate authority, also distanced her from any immediate competition with Jean.

It was then almost inevitable that Jeanne should act as the head of the anti-French party in initiating the diplomatic shift that followed the royal sentence. She clearly outranked the rest of the regional nobility, and so where Froissart had listed the Bretons and then Jeanne, for Le Grant she took precedence. Moreover, she did not merely agree in spirit with the rest of the regional elites, but took action, first receiving her envoys' reports and then sending for Duke Jean to return from England. She was thus pivotal in transforming a legal objection into an outright rebellion. This hierarchy and initiative were also reinforced when the viscount of Rohan brought news of the king's military plans back to Jeanne and the "other" nobles of Brittany. She took counsel with them and together they began to assemble an army to defend their Breton homeland and its liberties. With this portrayal, Le Grant turned Jeanne into Jean's lieutenant, exercising power in his absence but towards the same ends. Ultimately, she relied on his return, but was also the one who made it possible in the first place.

Having successfully recalled her cousin to power, Jeanne consolidated her place as first among his supporters. This dynamic played out most dramatically in a scene that was at once derivative and unique.[127] Jean celebrated his return from exile by disembarking at the northern town of Dinan (a ducal holding in the heart of Penthièvre territory), where he first delivered a speech to "his" Bretons, criticizing the king's usurpation and praising Brittany's historical greatness and privileges. He then retreated to a more private space in the local Dominican friary to reiterate his justifications in greater technical detail. Jeanne, as first to respond within this assembled inner circle (*ceteros precedere*), reprised her position of command among the ducal advisors seen in the chivalric chronicles. In fact, the speech Le Grant put into her mouth was taken from a foundational piece of Arthurian lore, Geoffrey of Monmouth's enormously influential *Historia Regum Britannie.* This early twelfth-century work helped define King Arthur's role in British history (comprising both Great Britain and Armorican Brittany), and Le Grant had used it to develop much of the earlier period of his chronicle. By returning to this material out-of-context, however, he set Jeanne and Jean's dynamic into a well-known mould.

Monmouth's original speech was delivered by Hoël, king of Brittany, to his cousin Arthur, when Arthur's lands and sovereignty were being threat-

127 BnF, MS lat. 6003, fol. 109r.

ened by the Romans.[128] The parallels with Jeanne's situation in the *Chronicon Briocense* were obvious, as Le Grant reminded the reader that Jeanne was Jean's first cousin and called her "Jeanne de Bretagne, countess of Penthièvre," marking her out as a Breton ruler but a subordinate one like Hoël. Hoël's speech had three main parts.[129] First, he praised Arthur's wisdom and the solidarity of his advisors. He then expressed confidence in their prospects of victory against Rome in a righteous cause, justifying Arthur's offensive measures as a licit response to attempted theft. Finally, he confirmed that fate and God were on their side and pledged all their lives to Arthur's war, specifically offering to stand with him with ten thousand warriors. The appeal of these themes in Jeanne's reconciliation with Jean are readily apparent. This speech made her acknowledge Jean's worthiness as a leader, transferring to him all the legitimacy—personal, legal, and divine—she might once have claimed for herself and/or her husband.

In giving these words to Jeanne, Le Grant made some necessary contextual changes, substituting the regions of France for Rome, playing up the Breton–French conflict, and removing references to classical rhetoric and prophecy. He also made three smaller edits that underscored different aspects of Jeanne's relationship with Jean. In the first two sections, Hoël's use of the second person singular *tu* to refer to Arthur gave way to Jeanne's use of the plural *vous*, displaying a greater degree of respect and hierarchy.[130] Nevertheless, rather than protecting only their liberties, they now defended their *patria*, their homeland—or inheritance. As Bretons, Jeanne and Jean shared a common stake, effectively burying the memory of the disputed succession. At the end, Jeanne offered Jean not a clearly enumerated force, but "'all the strength of arms of my territory'" (*omnem vim armatam territorii mei*). This localization of her military might confirmed that she did not control the entire duchy, but also reinforced her independent right of command in a lesser capacity. She could therefore function as Jean's partner, not in the sense of being his equal, but as an active participant in his rule. This partnership was apparent to the assembled barons, who responded to Jeanne's inspirational words by "praising and approving the duke and countess and joining them" in the fight.[131]

128 Monmouth, *History of the Kings of Britain*, para. 160.

129 Cf. Martin, "Hoel-Hearted Loyalty," 32.

130 Cf. above, p. 77.

131 "Ipsorum ducis et comitisse laudantes et approbantes et eis adherentes."

The choice of Hoël as a prototype for Jeanne reflects how her involvement in the rebellion was not primarily interpreted with reference to a marked gender. Both her leadership and her subordination came as a function of her rank and lineage, rather than on her capacity as a woman. She organized legal, diplomatic, and finally martial activities with equal competence and lack of fuss. Perhaps the only concession to the limits of her potential was that she did not, unlike Hoël, offer to stand beside Jean in person, but her absence in no way detracted from the military importance of her contribution. On the contrary, she was an exemplar to the rest of the barons, who immediately followed her model (*ad instar...huius domine comitisse*) in pledging troops to the duke. Jeanne's ability to unify and motivate the regional nobility into war made her a natural participant in a scene originally constructed around men alone.

The Arthurian echoes would have been apparent to much of Le Grant's intended audience, given the popularity of Monmouth's story and its many derivatives. However, they did not appeal to any of Le Grant's successors, for the memory of Jeanne's activity in 1379 waned in the later fifteenth-century accounts. Following Froissart, Le Baud's *Compillation* listed Jeanne de Bretagne, countess of Penthièvre and wife of Charles de Blois, among the duke's partisans. He cited personal motivations only: the devastation of civil war was preventing her from peaceably enjoying her lands.[132] Her stakes remained safely local, reflecting concerns that any regional aristocrat might reasonably have. He repeated this story in his *Histoire*, but without explaining why the countess acted as she did.[133] However, this time he had also taken inspiration from Le Grant (though citing Saint-André) to report that the countess had defended her cousin's rights in the royal court, followed secondarily by her own. Le Baud was therefore willing to recognize Jeanne's contribution on the basis of the promises made at the conclusion of the war, but he did not go so far as Le Grant in making her Jean's right-hand woman. At the same time, he noted that the king of France continued to refer to Jeanne as duchess of Brittany (while denying Duke Jean his own title), a clearly improper usage. On this point, Bouchart was more neutral, keeping verbatim Jeanne's title as duchess of Brittany in the second treaty of Guérande, which he quoted at length.[134] But he chose not to keep any of Jeanne's activity in the lead-up to this settlement, leaving her the passive

132 LBC, 424.

133 LBH, 361–62.

134 GCB, 2:144, 147; Morice, ed., *Mémoires*, 2:299, 301.

recipient of a deal worked out between duke and king. This omission probably had less to do with Jeanne herself than with Bouchart's pro-French interest in downplaying the attempted annexation as a whole.[135] Le Grant's satisfying resolution to the original Penthièvre–Montfort rift, reconciling Jean and Jeanne in an archetype of dynastic harmony, had its moment, but later gave way to other concerns.

Conclusions

To the extent that she was able to nurture rather than challenge family interests, Jeanne could occupy a satisfactory function within its history, whereas Charles's pursuit of the war led to undesirable outcomes and even undermined his masculinity both as a duke and as paterfamilias. Conversely, when it was Jeanne who chased the ducal title, she showcased the inadvisability of female authority—although maintaining and transmitting her rightful patrimony to her own line remained acceptable—while Charles became either a paragon or, paradoxically, a victim of her usurpation. The development of these dynamics in both Le Baud's and Bouchart's works never rose to the level of highly gendered praise or condemnation that we sometimes find in more polemic assessments of medieval rulers. Without denying that such extreme indictments certainly existed, there is a historiographical overrepresentation of slanderous reputations, which can lend disproportionate weight to highly polarized readings of gendered rulership. The Montfortists' more moderate and ambivalent reactions to the civil war remind us that the foundations of aristocratic partnerships complicated any uniform approach to the strategic deployment of masculinized and feminized ideals.

At the same time, while there is considerable overlap between these chronicles and their predecessors, Le Baud and Bouchart heightened Jeanne's and Charles's structural individuality. Whereas Froissart and even Cuvelier largely framed their partnership as functioning in tandem, now there was greater emphasis on the potential for difference and even opposition. This approach gave the Montfortist historians greater leeway in placing the Penthièvre leaders within the dynasty's vertical framework in order to address questions of its long-term unitary integrity. Their solutions generally represented familial authority using only one member of the couple at a time, creating a transmission of power concentrated in a single person rather than in a pair. Nevertheless, such strategies of inclusion and exclu-

135 Guitton, "Vices des princes," 464–65.

sion fundamentally relied on the possibility of shared power. Legitimating and de-legitimating different aspects of Jeanne's and Charles's authority by turns necessarily gave them both an active part in the processes of leadership, even if it did not establish clear parameters for how such collaborative authority should operate. The resulting narrative instability indicates that the unilateral model of power was not self-evident. Rather, these authors asserted that model against a persistently viable alternative of power-sharing as a solution to dynastic challenges. Framing the Breton civil war as a discrete conflict that marked a turning-point in how ducal power was organized suggested that a definitive configuration was possible, but the prevailing conditions of constant crisis made revisiting the issue of leadership almost inevitable.

CONCLUSION

IN THIS CASE study, I examined the evolution of Jeanne's and Charles's *fama* on three levels to show how reputation was constructed in different written contexts, and how historians can understand these texts as sources for reputation. The first level distinguished three major narrative phases: the papal inquiry into Charles's canonization, the French chivalric chronicles, and the Breton dynastic histories. The second level played out in the revisions produced by the same author, their continuators, or, for the canonization, by reworking spoken testimony into official record. The third level comprised the detailed variations between individual witnesses (human or manuscript). This multilayered heterogeneity encourages us to think about the norms of power, gender, and reputation as arguments rather than benchmarks, questions rather than answers.

At the first level, I showed how different aims and audiences meant prioritizing specific reputational traits, alongside the relative distribution of leadership within an aristocratic partnership. The proponents of Charles's canonization confronted the complications of lordship during a civil war by establishing his martial masculinity through less violent, even anti-knightly means. Jeanne, although not the focus of that inquiry, provided a useful reference point for the normal parameters of seigneurial authority and spousal responsibilities. Conversely, the chivalric chroniclers commended Jeanne's and Charles's exemplary courtliness and conduct of warfare, incorporating both princes into the paradigm of the martial nobility for whom they wrote. The ducal partnership was built out of their distinct but complementary identities and relationships, and the ability to mutually delegate power to each other. Finally, the Montfortist writers emphasized greater distinctions in the balance of responsibility, in order to mitigate the risks of female succession in light of the challenges facing their ducal patrons. They refrained, however, from developing a particularly negative view of Jeanne's leadership because she was easier to integrate within the all-important dynastic fold.

The developments from version to version within each phase clarified how even written reputations took part in an ongoing debate. At one end of the spectrum, the schematic template of sainthood that was imposed retroactively on the collected canonization testimony created a gloss of artificial unity beyond that achieved by the original questioning process. By contrast, Froissart's re-writing of the war did not tend towards any one direction, but experimented continually with the different possibilities of the affective and hierarchical modes of leadership familiar to his audience. Somewhere in the middle, Cuvelier's prose adaptations and the Montfortists reworked specific aspects of the received narrative tradition, supplemented with their own inventions, but were not necessarily internally coherent.

Within the fine-grained level, the real dynamism of reputation became even more complicated. The individual testimony from Charles's associates deployed many different strategies for rationalizing his exceptional leadership, such that witnesses contradicted each other at points. Jeanne could—or could not—share in Charles's pious fortitude; Charles did—or did not—make concessions to normative princely behaviour to uphold his responsibilities to his wife. The reinterpretation of Jeanne's pursuit of her claims as unwarranted aggression, featured in only a handful of Froissart manuscripts but perpetuated and embellished by the later Montfortists, was largely a function of the extent to which any given account wanted to accept Charles's virtue.

The variability evident within this case study underscores the value of a critical approach to reputation as it turned people into personas and events into history. Studying reputation lets us examine which stories elites chose to tell about themselves, why and how they told them, and what those decisions say about their socio-political environment. This process mattered just as much as "what actually happened" because controlling the narrative is fundamental to shaping the relations of power within a society. If the history of political action deals with "the players of the game," the history of political culture asks "what the players presume the nature and limits of their game to be."[1] The repeated representation and commemoration of powerful individuals reflected, and influenced, those presumptions. Nevertheless, we have seen that reputations became more diffuse as the number of interpretations grew. People in medieval societies (like any other) had diverse opinions on gender, authority, and violence—and even a single narrator might change their story under other circumstances. The political culture of the medieval aristocracy, then, emerged from the opposing forces of consolidation and variegation. Because there was never a stable or complete consensus on the rules of a game rife with double standards, constructing

1 Hoak, introduction to *Tudor Political Culture*, 1.

reputation was essentially a sales pitch, aiming to get others to buy in to a given model. Reputation thus offers a window onto the continuous renegotiation of a range of cultural and analytical touchstones, including superficially binary categories such as sacred and secular, masculine and feminine, or war and peace, as well as equally superficial monoliths such as chivalry, lordship, sanctity, and lineage.

This perspective also underscores a number of disparities between premodern depictions of collaborative power and modern treatments of this dynamic. Negative reputations, especially of women, have often drawn much greater attention than positive ones. Reducing legitimate rulership to a single actor has obscured the salience of male/female co-rulership in earlier thought. Shared power could as readily be seen as a solution to contested authority as its cause. And the often-formulaic preoccupations of medieval history-writers did not preclude significant versatility in the templates they applied to enhance or downplay partnership. Embracing the complexity of reputation therefore sheds light on the complexity of the political societies it helped support and regulate.

I introduced the concept of relational reputations to draw attention to the importance of partnerships in this discursive process. First, reputation was determined and communicated not simply according to whatever set of standards was thought best to apply, but in comparison to how others achieved or deviated from the ideal. The spousal relationship heightened such parallels and contrasts by building in an immediate counterpart and facilitating the interplay of archetypes between the two. This connection also cut across gendered lines in a way that most other points of reference tended not to, potentially engaging a broader spectrum of norms in the process. Second, commentators passed value judgements not only on each half of the couple, but on the nature of their partnership itself. Being of good or ill repute depended not on individual merit alone, but on how well they worked together in that context. This dynamic sharpened the focus of reputation by directing it at a concrete aim and demanding that it adapt to any new circumstances faced by the couple. Because relational reputations incorporated multiple moving parts, they served as a powerful tool of political critique, and deserve greater attention in our analyses of men's and women's authority in premodern political culture.

At the same time, if the specific implementation of reputational categories depended on the agendas of the moment, the very fact of working through them over and over again ultimately reinforced the terms on which legitimate political authority was evaluated. In other words, the expectations of gender, leadership, and relationships were never one-size-fits all, but there consistently *were* such expectations. The proof of holiness may have sometimes stemmed from, and sometimes substituted for, the performance of seigneurial knighthood; but either way, sanctity was construed rather more symbiotically with lordship than it might first appear. The respective contributions by each half of a ruling couple to the projects of governance and violence were subjective and even open to wildly divergent value judgements; but the partnership itself remained salient as an integral part of interpreting the nature of their authority as well as a vehicle for bigger narratives about the historical significance of a given reign. The gendering of individuals was not a predetermined or fixed trait, but was continually assessed through their actions in relation to others, even as the essential relevance of gender, and indeed the overall presumption of masculine dominance, went largely unquestioned. Finally, loyalty was determined not only by the bond between leader and follower, but by the networks in which each was enmeshed and which helped identify every power-holder by their place in the wider scheme of things. The more things change, the more they stay the same.

The process of constructing reputation on the basis of such frameworks confirmed the parameters for recognizing political legitimacy, without reifying legitimacy itself as an objective, persistent asset. Instead, the active discourse provoked by contested legitimacy gave these norms the flexible resilience they needed to stay relevant over the long term. More rigid expectations of aristocratic partnerships and gendered authority responded poorly to the pressures of constant crisis, which demanded continual efforts to define who was and was not allowed to wield violence and uphold order. Deploying instead both positive and negative models of martial leadership, and for women and men simultaneously, made it easier to manage the messy hierarchies and associations within the nobility, and gave seigneurial power the gloss of regulation along with considerable plasticity in implementation. These versatile dynamics can help explain how European aristocracies maintained their hegemony despite significant regional variation and ongoing challenges across the medieval and early modern periods.

BIBLIOGRAPHY

Manuscript and Archival Material

Besançon, Bibliothèque municipale, MS 865*.

Chicago, Newberry Library, MS Case f.37.2*.

Nantes, Archives départementales de Loire-Atlantique, E 6-4.

Oxford, Bodleian Library, Laud misc. 745*.

Paris, Bibliothèque nationale de France, MSS français 2640, 2647, 2650*, 2677.

Paris, Bibliothèque nationale de France, MS latin 6003.

*Transcriptions consulted via Peter Ainsworth and Godfried Croenen, eds. *The Online Froissart*, v.1.5. HRIOnline, 2013. https://www.dhi.ac.uk/onlinefroissart/.

Printed Editions and Translations

Bouchart, Alain. *Les grandes croniques de Bretaigne*. Edited by Marie-Louise Auger, Gustave Jeanneau, and Bernard Guenée. 2 vols. Centre national de la recherche scientifique, 1998.

Buchon, J.-A.-C., ed. "Chronique anonyme de sire Bertrand du Guesclin." In *Choix de chroniques et mémoires sur l'histoire de France*, 4:1–95. Desrez, 1839.

Cuvelier. *La chanson de Bertrand du Guesclin de Cuvelier*. Edited by Jean-Claude Faucon. 3 vols. Éditions universitaires du Sud, 1990.

——. *The Song of Bertrand du Guesclin*. Translated by Nigel Bryant. Boydell, 2019.

Delachenal, R., ed. *Les grandes chroniques de France: Chronique des règnes de Jean II et de Charles V*. 4 vols. Renouard, 1910–1920.

Froissart, Jean. *Chroniques: Dernière rédaction du premier livre, édition du manuscrit de Rome Reg. lat. 869*. Edited by George T. Diller. Droz, 1972.

——. *Chroniques: Livre I, le manuscrit d'Amiens*. Edited by George T. Diller. 5 vols. Droz, 1991–1998.

——. *Chroniques de J. Froissart*. Edited by Siméon Luce. 11 vols. Renouard, 1869–1899.

——. *Œuvres de Froissart: Chroniques*. Edited by J.-B.-M.-C. Kervyn de Lettenhove. 25 vols. Devaux, 1867–1877.

Géraud, Hercule, ed. *Chronique latine de Guillaume de Nangis de 1113 à 1300, avec les continuations de cette chronique de 1300 à 1368*. 2 vols. Renouard, 1843.

Graham-Goering, Erika, Michael Jones, and Bertrand Yeurc'h, eds. *Aux origines de la guerre de succession de Bretagne: Documents (1341–1342)*. Presses universitaires de Rennes, 2019.

Héry, Laurent, Jean-Paul Le Guillou, Yves Le Guillou, Armelle Le Huërou, and André Vauchez, eds. *Le procès de canonisation de Charles de Blois, duc de Bretagne (1319–1364)*. Vol. 1, *Le procès d'Angers (1371)*. Presses universitaires de Rennes, 2023.

Jones, Michael, ed. *Recueil des actes de Charles de Blois et Jeanne de Penthièvre, duc et duchesse de Bretagne (1341–1364), suivi des actes de Jeanne de Penthièvre (1364–1384)*. 1996. Presses universitaires de Rennes, 2016. https://books.openedition.org/pur/28420.

——, ed. *Recueil des actes de Jean IV, duc de Bretagne*. 2 vols. Klincksieck, 1980–2001.

La Borderie, Arthur Le Moyne de, ed. *Inventaire du mobilier de Jeanne la Boîteuse, duchesse de Bretagne (1384)*. Guéraud, 1854.

Le Baud, Pierre. *Compillation des cronicques et ystoires des Bretons*. Edited by Karine Abélard. Presses universitaires de Rennes, 2018.

——. "La '*Genealogie des roys, ducs et princes de Bretaigne*' de Pierre Le Baud (1486)," edited by Jean Kerhervé. In *Bretagne et pays celtiques: Langues, histoire, civilisation. Mélanges offerts à la mémoire de Léon Fleuriot*, edited by Gwennolé Le Menn and Jean-Yves Le Moing, 519–60. Presses universitaires de Rennes, 1992.

——. *Histoire de Bretagne, avec les chroniques des maisons de Vitré et de Laval*. Edited by C. d'Hosier. Alliot, 1638.

Le Bel, Jean. *Chronique de Jean Le Bel*. Edited by Jules Viard and Eugène Déprez. 2 vols. Renouard, 1904.

——. *The True Chronicles of Jean Le Bel, 1290–1360*. Translated by Nigel Bryant. Boydell, 2011.

[Le Fèvre, Jean?]. *Le songe du vergier*. Edited by Marion Schnerb-Lièvre. 2 vols. Centre national de la recherche scientifique, 1982.

[Le Grant, Hervé?]. *Chronicon Briocense: Chronique de Saint-Brieuc (fin 14e siècle), éditée et traduite d'après les manuscrits BN 6003–BN 8899*. Edited and translated by Gwenaël Le Duc and Claude Sterckx. Vol. 1. Simon, 1972.

Ménard, Claude, ed. *Histoire de messire Bertrand du Guesclin, connestable de France*. Cramoisy, 1618.

Molinier, Auguste, and Émile Molinier, eds. *Chronique normande du XIVe siècle*. Renouard, 1882.

Monmouth, Geoffrey of. *The History of the Kings of Britain*. Edited by Michael D. Reeve. Translated by Neil Wright. Boydell, 2007.

Moranvillé, H. *Chronographia regum Francorum*. 3 vols. Renouard, 1892–1897.

Morice, Hyacinthe, ed. *Mémoires pour servir de preuves à l'histoire ecclésiastique et civile de Bretagne*. 3 vols. Osmont, 1742–1746.

Pizan, Christine de. *Le livre des trois vertus*. Edited by Charity Cannon Willard. Champion, 1989.

Saint-André, Guillaume de. *Chronique de l'État breton*. Edited and translated by Jean-Michel Cauneau and Dominique Philippe. Presses universitaires de Rennes, 2005.

Saint-Paul, Jean de. *Chronique de Bretagne de Jean de Saint-Paul, chambellan du duc François II*. Edited by Arthur Le Moyne de La Borderie. Société des bibliophiles bretons et de l'histoire de Bretagne, 1881.

Sérent, Antoine de, ed. *Monuments du procès de canonisation du bienheureux Charles de Blois, duc de Bretagne, 1320–1364*. Prud'homme, 1921.

Viard, Jules, ed. *Les grandes chroniques de France*. 10 vols. Champion, 1920–1953.

Secondary Works

Adams, Tracy. *The Life and Afterlife of Isabeau of Bavaria*. Johns Hopkins University Press, 2010.

Ainsworth, Peter. "Contemporary and 'Eyewitness' History." In *Historiography in the Middle Ages*, edited by Deborah Mauskopf Deliyannis, 249–76. Brill, 2003.

——. "Froissardian Perspectives on Late-Fourteenth-Century Society." In *Orders and Hierarchies in Late Medieval and Renaissance Europe*, edited by Jeffrey Denton, 56–73. Macmillan, 1999.

——. "Froissart, Jean." In *Encyclopedia of the Medieval Chronicle*, edited by Graeme Dunphy, 642–45. 2010. Brill, 2021.

——. "Jean Froissart: Chronicler, Poet and Writer." In *The Online Froissart*, v.1.5, edited by Peter Ainsworth and Godfried Croenen. HRIOnline, 2013. https://www.dhi.ac.uk/onlinefroissart/.

——. *Jean Froissart and the Fabric of History: Truth, Myth, and Fiction in the Chroniques*. Clarendon, 1990.

Allirot, Anne-Hélène. "La *male royne boiteuse*: Jeanne de Bourgogne." In *Royautés imaginaires (XIIe–XVIe siècles)*, edited by Anne-Hélène Allirot, Gilles Lecuppre, and Lydwine Scordia, 119–33. Brepols, 2005.

Althoff, Gerd. *Family, Friends and Followers: Political and Social Bonds in Medieval Europe*. Translated by Christopher Carroll. Cambridge University Press, 2004.

Ambühl, Rémy. *Prisoners of War in the Hundred Years War: Ransom Culture in the Late Middle Ages*. Cambridge University Press, 2013.

Arbelet, François, and Marielle Devlaeminck, eds. "Fama: Réputation et renommée." *Questes* 42 (2021). https://journals.openedition.org/questes/5626.

Argentré, Bertrand d'. *L'histoire de Bretaigne*. Duclos, 1583.

Armstrong-Partida, Michelle. "Sex and Priestly Masculinity in Late Medieval Europe." In *Masculinités sacerdotales*, edited by Jean-Pascal Gay, Silvia Mostaccio, and Josselin Tricou, 251–78. Brepols, 2022.

Aurell, Martin. "Rapport introductif." In *Chevalerie et christianisme aux XIIe et XIIIe siècles*. Edited by Martin Aurell and Catalina Girbea, 12–48. Presses universitaires de Rennes, 2011.

Autrand, Françoise. "L'image de la noblesse en France à la fin du Moyen Âge: Tradition et nouveauté." *Comptes rendus des séances de l'Académie des inscriptions et belles-lettres* 123 (1979): 340–54.

Backerra, Charlotte. "Personal Union, Composite Monarchy and 'Multiple Rule.'" In *The Routledge History of Monarchy*, edited by Elena Woodacre, Lucinda H. S. Dean, Chris Jones, Russell E. Martin, and Zita Eva Rohr, 89–111. Routledge, 2019.

Bagerius, Henric, and Christine Ekholst. "For Better or for Worse: Royal Marital Sexuality as Political Critique in Late Medieval Europe." In *The Routledge History of Monarchy*, edited by Elena Woodacre, Lucinda H. S. Dean, Chris Jones, Russell E. Martin, and Zita Eva Rohr, 636–54. Routledge, 2019.

——. "The Unruly Queen: Blanche of Namur and Dysfunctional Rulership in Medieval Sweden." In *Queenship, Gender, and Reputation in the Medieval and Early Modern West, 1060–1600*, edited by Zita Eva Rohr and Lisa Benz, 99–118. Palgrave Macmillan, 2016.

Barton, Richard E. "'Zealous Anger' and the Renegotiation of Aristocratic Relationships in Eleventh- and Twelfth-Century France." In *Anger's Past: The Social Uses of an Emotion in the Middle Ages*, edited by Barbara H. Rosenwein, 153–70. Cornell University Press, 1998.

Bateman, Mary. "Knight Fever: Sickness, Masculinity and Narrative Absence in the *Mort Artu*, Béroul's *Tristan* and Thomas of Britain's *Tristan*." *Journal of the International Arthurian Society* 9 (2021): 36–62.

Beem, Charles, and Miles Taylor, eds. *The Man Behind the Queen: Male Consorts in History*. Palgrave Macmillan, 2014.

Benz, Lisa. "Conspiracy and Alienation: Queen Margaret of France and Piers Gaveston, the King's Favorite." In *Queenship, Gender, and Reputation in the Medieval and Early Modern West, 1060–1600*, edited by Zita Eva Rohr and Lisa Benz, 119–41. Palgrave Macmillan, 2016.

Benz St. John, Lisa. *Three Medieval Queens: Queenship and the Crown in Fourteenth-Century England*. Palgrave Macmillan, 2012.

Bisson, Thomas N., Dominique Barthélemy, Stephen D. White, Timothy Reuter, and Chris Wickham. "Debate: The 'Feudal Revolution.'" *Past & Present* 142 (1994): 6–42; 152 (1996): 197–223; 155 (1997): 177–225.

Blincoe, Mark E. "Geoffrey le Bel of Anjou and Political Inheritance in the Anglo-Norman Realm." *Haskins Society Journal* 27 (2016): 79–100.

Bolton, Brenda, and Christine Meek, eds. *Aspects of Power and Authority in the Middle Ages*. Brepols, 2007.

Boquet, Damien, and Piroska Nagy. *Medieval Sensibilities: A History of Emotions in the Middle Ages*. Translated by Robert Shaw. Polity Press, 2018.

Boston, H. C. *Lordship and Locality in the Long Twelfth Century*. Boydell, 2024.

Boulet, Noël Maurice-Denis. "La canonisation de Charles de Blois (1376)." *Revue d'histoire de l'Église de France* 28 (1942): 217–24.

Brero, Thalia, Frederik Buylaert, and Erika Graham-Goering. "Dynasties and Dynastic Rule between Elite Reproduction and State Building in Europe." In *Unions and Divisions: New Forms of Rule in Late Medieval Europe*, edited by Paul Srodecki, Norbert Kersken, and Rimvydas Petrauskas, 40–52. Routledge, 2023.

Broomhall, Susan. "Introduction—Destroying Order, Structuring Disorder: Gender and Emotions." In *Gender and Emotions in Medieval and Early Modern Europe: Destroying Order, Structuring Disorder*, edited by Susan Broomhall, 1–13. Routledge, 2015.

Brown, Cynthia J., ed. *The Cultural and Political Legacy of Anne de Bretagne: Negotiating Convention in Books and Documents*. Brewer, 2010.

Brown, Elizabeth A. R., and Richard C. Famiglietti. *The Lit de Justice: Semantics, Ceremonial, and the Parlement of Paris 1300–1600*. Thorbecke, 1994.

Brundage, James A. *Law, Sex, and Christian Society in Medieval Europe*. University of Chicago Press, 1987.

Bruso, Steven. "Bodies Hardened for War: Knighthood in Fifteenth-Century England." *Journal of Medieval and Early Modern Studies* 47 (2017): 255–77.

Burnley, David. *Courtliness and Literature in Medieval England*. Longman, 1998.

Carré, Yannick. *Le baiser sur la bouche au Moyen Âge: Rites, symboles, mentalités, XIe–XVe siècles*. Léopard d'Or, 1992.

Casey, Jim. "Feeling It Like a Man: Masculine Grief in Medieval and Early Modern Texts." In *Grief, Gender, and Identity in the Middle Ages: Knowing Sorrow*, edited by Lee Templeton, 234–57. Brill, 2022.

Cassard, Jean-Christophe. *Charles de Blois (1319–1364): Duc de Bretagne et bienheureux*. Centre de recherche bretonne et celtique, 1994.

——. "Les coulisses de la sainteté? Charles de Blois vu par son entourage." *Annales de Bretagne et des Pays de l'Ouest* 116, no. 1 (2009): 183–96.

——. "Les *Gestes des Bretons en Italie* ou le voyage sans la découverte." In *1491: La Bretagne, terre d'Europe*, edited by Jean Kerhervé and Tanguy Daniel, 101–17. Centre de recherche bretonne et celtique, 1992.

——. *La guerre de succession de Bretagne*. Coop Breizh, 2006.

——. "Un historien au travail: Pierre Le Baud." *Mémoires de la Société d'histoire et d'archéologie de Bretagne* 62 (1985): 67–95.

——. "La *patience* du duc Charles cartographiée: Son intérêt historique." In *Corona monastica: Moines bretons de Landévennec. Histoire et mémoire celtiques*, edited by Louis Lemoine and Bernard Merdrignac, 289–98. Presses universitaires de Rennes, 2004.

Challet, Vincent. "Violence as a Political Language: The Uses and Misuses of Violence in Late Medieval French and English Popular Rebellions." In *The Routledge History Handbook of Medieval Revolt*, edited by Justine Firnhaber-Baker and Dirk Schoenaers, 279–91. Routledge, 2017.

Chareyron, Nicole. *Jean Le Bel: Le maître de Froissart, grand imagier de la guerre de Cent Ans*. De Boeck, 1996.

Chassel, Jean-Luc. "Le nom et les armes: La matrilinéarité dans la parenté aristocratique du second Moyen Âge." *Droit et cultures* 64 (2012): 117–48.

Coativy, Yves, and Anne Massoni, eds. "La vicomté de Limoges sous les ducs de Bretagne." Special issue, *Annales de Bretagne et des Pays de l'Ouest* 126, no. 2 (2019).

Coleman, Janet. "Scholastic Treatments of Maintaining One's *Fama* (Reputation/Good Name) and the Correction of Private 'Passions' for the Public Good and Public Legitimacy." *Cultural and Social History* 2 (2005): 23–48.

Comaroff, John. "Reflections on the Political Theology of Conflict: From Medieval Scandinavia to the Global Future." In *Medieval and Modern Civil Wars: A Comparative Perspective*, edited by Jón Viðar Sigurðsson and Hans Jacob Orning, 279–308. Brill, 2021.

Constable, Giles. "Attitudes Toward Self-Inflicted Suffering in the Middle Ages." The Ninth Stephen J. Brademas, Sr., Lecture. Hellenic College Press, 1982.

Contamine, Philippe. "En marge d'une grande édition: La biographie de Bertrand du Guesclin insérée dans la *Chronographia regum Francorum*." In *Guerres, voyages et quêtes au Moyen Âge: Mélanges offertes à Jean-Claude Faucon*, edited by Alain Labbé, Daniel Lacroix, and Danielle Quéruel, 103–10. Champion, 2000.

——. "Points de vue sur la chevalerie en France à la fin du Moyen Âge." *Francia* 4 (1976): 255–85.

"La coseigneurie." Special issue, *Mélanges de l'École française de Rome – Moyen Âge* 122, no. 1 (2010). https://journals.openedition.org/mefrm/589.

Coulton, George Gordon. *The Chronicler of European Chivalry*. Studio, 1930.

Courroux, Pierre. *L'écriture de l'histoire dans les chroniques françaises (XIIe–XVe siècle)*. Garnier, 2016.

Croenen, Godfried. "Froissart et ses mécènes: Quelques problèmes biographiques." In *Froissart dans sa forge*, edited by Odile Bombarde, 9–32. Académie des inscriptions et belles-lettres, 2006.

——. "La guerre en Normandie au XIVe siècle et le problème de l'évolution textuelle des *Chroniques* de Jean Froissart." In *La guerre en Normandie (XIe–XVe siècle)*, edited by Anne Curry and Véronique Gazeau, 111–47. Presses universitaires de Caen, 2018.

——. "Jean Le Bel." In *Encyclopedia of the Medieval Chronicle*, edited by Graeme Dunphy, 913–14. 2010. Brill, 2021.

——. "Paris, Bibliothèque nationale de France, manuscrits *[sic]* français 2640." In *The Online Froissart*, v.1.5, edited by Peter Ainsworth and Godfried Croenen. HRIOnline, 2013. https://www.dhi.ac.uk/onlinefroissart/.

——. "The Reception of Froissart's Writings in England: The Evidence of the Manuscripts." In *Language and Culture in Medieval Britain: The French of England, c. 1100–c. 1500*, edited by Jocelyn Wogan-Browne, 409–19. York Medieval Press, 2009.

Crouch, David. *The Chivalric Turn: Conduct and Hegemony in Europe before 1300.* Oxford University Press, 2019.

Cullum, P. H. "Introduction: Holiness and Masculinity in Medieval Europe." In *Holiness and Masculinity in the Middle Ages*, edited by P. H. Cullum and Katherine J. Lewis, 1–7. University of Wales Press, 2004.

Davies, R. R. *Lords and Lordship in the British Isles in the Late Middle Ages.* Edited by Brendan Smith. Oxford University Press, 2009.

Débax, Hélène. *La seigneurie collective. Pairs, pariers, paratge: Les coseigneurs du XIe au XIIIe siècle.* Presses universitaires de Rennes, 2012.

Desmichels, C. *Tableau chronologique de l'histoire du Moyen Âge.* Colas, 1823.

Downes, Stephanie, Andrew Lynch, and Katrina O'Loughlin. "Introduction—War as Emotion: Cultural Fields of Conflict and Feeling." In *Emotions and War: Medieval to Romantic Literature*, edited by Stephanie Downes, Andrew Lynch, and Katrina O'Loughlin, 1–23. Palgrave Macmillan, 2015.

Dressler, Rachel. "Steel Corpse: Imaging the Knight in Death." In *Conflicted Identities and Multiple Masculinities: Men in the Medieval West*, edited by Jacqueline Murray, 135–67. 1999. Routledge, 2011.

Duch, Anna. "Chasing St Louis: The English Monarchy's Pursuit of Sainthood." In *The Routledge History of Monarchy*, edited by Elena Woodacre, Lucinda H. S. Dean, Chris Jones, Russell E. Martin, and Zita Eva Rohr, 330–51. Routledge, 2019.

Duindam, Jeroen. "Gender, Succession and Dynastic Rule." *History and Anthropology* 32 (2021): 151–70.

Dumolyn, Jan, Jelle Haemers, Hipólito Rafael Oliva Herrer, and Vincent Challet, eds. *The Voices of the People in Late Medieval Europe: Communication and Popular Politics.* Brepols, 2014.

Earenfight, Theresa. "Without the Persona of the Prince: Kings, Queens and the Idea of Monarchy in Late Medieval Europe." *Gender & History* 19 (2007): 1–21.

Elukin, Jonathan M. "Warrior or Saint? Joinville, Louis IX's Character, and the Challenge of the Crusade." In *Center and Periphery: Studies on Power in the Medieval World in Honor of William Chester Jordan*, edited by Katherine L. Jansen, G. Geltner, and Anne E. Lester, 183–94. Brill, 2013.

Esmark, Kim, Lars Hermanson, and Hans Jacob Orning, eds. *Nordic Elites in Transformation, c. 1050–1250.* Vol. 2, *Social Networks.* Routledge, 2020.

Estourbeillon, Régis de l'. *Le serment de Jean de Lesnerac, meurtrier de Charles de Blois.* Prud'homme, 1896.

Everard, Judith. "Sworn Testimony and Memory of the Past in Brittany, c.1100–1250." In *Medieval Memories: Men, Women and the Past, 700–1300*, edited by Elisabeth van Houts, 72–91. Pearson, 2001.

Evergates, Theodore. *The Aristocracy in the County of Champagne: 1100–1300*. University of Pennsylvania Press, 2007.

Fenster, Thelma, and Daniel Lord Smail, eds. *Fama: The Politics of Talk and Reputation in Medieval Europe*. Cornell University Press, 2003.

Firnhaber-Baker, Justine. *Violence and the State in Languedoc, 1250–1400*. Cambridge University Press, 2014.

Flannery, Mary C., and Katie L. Walter, eds. *The Culture of Inquisition in Medieval England*. Cambridge University Press, 2013.

Fletcher, Christopher. "Introduction: Masculinity and *Politik*." In *The Palgrave Handbook of Masculinity and Political Culture in Europe*, edited by Christopher Fletcher, Sean Brady, Rachel E. Moss, and Lucy Riall, 1–16. Palgrave Macmillan, 2018.

——. *Richard II: Manhood, Youth, and Politics, 1377–99*. Oxford University Press, 2008.

Gaposchkin, M. Cecilia. *The Making of Saint Louis: Kingship, Sanctity, and Crusade in the Later Middle Ages*. Cornell University Press, 2008.

Gauvard, Claude. "*Fama* explicite et *fama* implicite: Les difficultés de l'historien face à l'honneur des petites gens aux derniers siècles du Moyen Âge." In *La légitimité implicite*, edited by Jean-Philippe Genet, 2:39–55. Éditions de la Sorbonne, 2015.

——, ed. "La renommée." Special issue, *Médiévales* 24 (1993).

——. "Les révoltes du règne de Charles VI: Tentatives pour expliquer un échec." In *Révolte et société*, edited by Fabienne Gambrelle and Michel Trebitsch, 1:53–61. Histoire au présent, 1989.

Genet, Jean-Philippe. "The Government of Later Medieval France and England: A Plea for Comparative History." In *Government and Political Life in England and France, c. 1300–c. 1500*, edited by Christopher Fletcher, Jean-Philippe Genet, and John Watts, 1–23. Cambridge University Press, 2015.

——. "Political Society and the Late Medieval State." In *New Approaches to the History of Late Medieval and Early Modern Europe*, edited by Troels Dahlerup and Per Ingesman, 11–36. Kongelige Danske Videnskabernes Selskab, 2009.

——. "Pouvoir symbolique, légitimation et genèse de l'État moderne." In *La légitimité implicite*, edited by Jean-Philippe Genet, 1:9–48. Éditions de la Sorbonne, 2015.

Gibbons, Rachel. "Isabeau of Bavaria, Queen of France (1385–1422): The Creation of an Historical Villainess." *Transactions of the Royal Historical Society*, 6th ser., 6 (1996): 51–73.

Gicquel, Yvonig. "Jean II de Rohan, grand competiteur à la couronne de Bretagne." *Bulletin de la Société d'archéologie et d'histoire du Pays de Lorient* 25 (1994): 5–13.

Goodich, Michael E. *Lives and Miracles of the Saints: Studies in Medieval Latin Hagiography*. Ashgate, 2004.

Graham-Goering, Erika. "Authority, Reputation, and the Roles of Jeanne de Penthièvre in Book I of Froissart's *Chroniques*." *Journal of Medieval History* 45 (2019): 100–127.

——. "Empowering Lordship in the Registers of Homage to Charles VI (Languedoc, 1389–1390)." *French Historical Studies* 45 (2022): 381–413.

——. *Princely Power in Late Medieval France: Jeanne de Penthièvre and the War for Brittany*. Cambridge University Press, 2020.

——. "Une principauté décentrée? Perspectives offertes par la vicomté de Limoges à partir de 1341." In *Gouverner et administrer les principautés des Alpes aux Pyrénées (XIIIe–début XVIe siècle)*, edited by Dominique Bidot-Germa, Pierre Courroux, and Véronique Lamazou-Duplan, 133–46. Ausonius, 2023.

Graham-Goering, Erika, Jim van der Meulen, and Frederik Buylaert, eds. *Lordship and the Decentralized State in Late Medieval Europe*. British Academy, 2025.

Green, David. "'A Woman Given to Slippery Ways'? The Reputation of Joan, the Fair Maid of Kent." In *People, Power and Identity in the Late Middle Ages: Essays in Memory of W. Mark Ormrod*, edited by Gwilym Dodd, Helen Lacey, and Anthony Musson, 305–23. Routledge, 2021.

Guay, Manuel. "Les émotions dans les cours princières au XVe siècle: Entre manifestations publiques et secret." *Questes* 16 (2009): 39–50.

Guenée, Bernard. *Du Guesclin et Froissart: La fabrication de la renommée*. Tallandier, 2008.

——. *L'opinion publique à la fin du Moyen Âge, d'après la "Chronique de Charles VI" du Religieux de Saint-Denis*. Perrin, 2002.

Guitton, Laurent. "Les vices des princes de Caligula à Louis XI: La construction d'un anti-modèle de souverain par les lettrés de la cour de Bretagne à la fin du Moyen Âge." In *La pathologie du pouvoir: Vices, crimes et délits des gouvernants*, edited by Patrick Gilli, 450–84. Brill, 2016.

Hadley, D. M., ed. *Masculinity in Medieval Europe*. Routledge, 1999.

Hardy, Duncan. *Associative Political Culture in the Holy Roman Empire: Upper Germany, 1346–1521*. Oxford University Press, 2018.

Harsgor, Mikhaël. "L'essor des bâtards nobles au XVe siècle." *Revue historique* 253 (1975): 319–54.

Harwood, Sophie. *Medieval Women and War: Female Roles in the Old French Tradition*. Bloomsbury, 2020.

Herrup, Cynthia. "The King's Two Genders." *Journal of British Studies* 45 (2006): 493–510.

Héry, Laurent. "De la guerre à la paix: Politique et sainteté dans la Bretagne ducale (1364–1442). Les cas de Charles de Blois et de Vincent Ferrier." *Annales de Bretagne et des Pays de l'Ouest* 129, no. 2 (2022): 9–27.

——. "Le culte de Charles de Blois: Résistances et réticences." *Annales de Bretagne et des Pays de l'Ouest* 103, no. 2 (1996): 39–56.

——. "La 'sainteté' de Charles de Blois: Vertus et virtus d'un duc de Bretagne." In *Corona monastica: Moines bretons de Landévennec. Histoire et mémoire celtiques*, edited by Louis Lemoine and Bernard Merdrignac, 299–309. Presses universitaires de Rennes, 2004.

——. "La 'sainteté' de Charles de Blois ou l'échec d'une entreprise de canonisation politique." *Britannia monastica* 10 (2006): 21–41.

Hoak, Dale. Introduction to *Tudor Political Culture*, 1–10. Cambridge University Press, 1995.

Hobbins, Daniel. *The Trial of Joan of Arc*. Harvard University Press, 2005.

Huneycutt, Lois L. "The Creation of a Crone: The Historical Reputation of Adelaide of Maurienne." In *Capetian Women*, edited by Kathleen Nolan, 27–43. Palgrave Macmillan, 2003.

——. "Intercession and the High-Medieval Queen: The Esther Topos." In *Power of the Weak: Studies on Medieval Women*, edited by Jennifer Carpenter and Sally-Beth MacLean, 126–46. University of Illinois Press, 1995.

Isaac, Steven. "Women in Command: The Matildine War of 1141." *War and Society* 41 (2022): 247–63.

Jones, Michael. "Ancenis, Froissart et le début de la guerre de succession en Bretagne (1341)." *Mémoires de la Société d'histoire et d'archéologie de Bretagne* 77 (1999): 91–102.

——. "Bouchart, Alain." In *Encyclopedia of the Medieval Chronicle*, edited by Graeme Dunphy, 194–95. 2010. Brill, 2021.

——. "The Breton Civil War." In *Froissart: Historian*, edited by J. J. N. Palmer, 64–81. Boydell, 1981.

——. *Ducal Brittany 1364–1399: Relations with England and France during the Reign of Duke John IV*. Oxford University Press, 1970.

——. "Marguerite de Clisson, comtesse de Penthièvre, et l'exercice du pouvoir." In *Femmes de pouvoir, femmes politiques durant les derniers siècles du Moyen Âge et au cours de la première Renaissance*, edited by Éric Bousmar, Jonathan Dumont, Alain Marchandisse and Bertrand Schnerb, 349–68. De Boeck, 2012.

——. "Politics, Sanctity and the Breton State: The Case of the Blessed Charles de Blois, Duke of Brittany (d. 1364)." In *The Medieval State: Essays Presented to James Campbell*, edited by J. R. Maddicott and D. M. Palliser, 215–32. Hambledon, 2000.

——. *Le premier inventaire du Trésor des chartes des ducs de Bretagne (1395): Hervé Le Grant et les origines du Chronicon Briocense*. Société d'histoire et d'archéologie de Bretagne, 2007.

Kantorowicz, Ernst A. *The King's Two Bodies: A Study in Mediaeval Political Theology*. Princeton University Press, 1957.

Karras, Ruth Mazo. *From Boys to Men: Formations of Masculinity in Late Medieval Europe*. University of Pennsylvania Press, 2003.

Karras, Ruth Mazo, and Katherine E. Pierpont. *Sexuality in Medieval Europe: Doing Unto Others*. 4th ed. Routledge, 2023.

Katajala-Peltomaa, Sari. *Gender, Miracles, and Daily Life: The Evidence of Fourteenth-Century Canonization Processes*. Brepols, 2009.

Kerhervé, Jean. "Aux origines d'un sentiment national: Les chroniqueurs bretons à la fin du Moyen Âge." *Bulletin de la Société archéologique du Finistère* 108 (1980): 165–206.

Klaniczay, Gábor. *Holy Rulers and Blessed Princesses: Dynastic Cults in Medieval Central Europe*. Translated by Éva Pálmai. Cambridge University Press, 2002.

Krötzl, Christian. "*Fama sanctitatis*: Die Akten der spätmittelalterlichen Kanonisationsprozesse als Quelle zu Kommunikation und Informationsvermittlung in der mittelalterlichen Gesellschaft." In *Procès de canonisation au Moyen Âge: Aspects juridiques et religieux*, edited by Gábor Klaniczay, 223–44. École française de Rome, 2004.

Krötzl, Christian, and Sari Katajala-Peltomaa. "Approaching Twelfth- to Fifteenth-Century Miracles: Miracle Registers, Collections, and Canonization Processes as Source Material." In *Miracles in Medieval Canonization Processes: Structures, Functions, and Methodologies*, edited by Christian Krötzl and Sari Katajala-Peltomaa, 1–39. Brepols, 2018.

Krynen, Jacques. "Naturel: Essai sur l'argument de la Nature dans la pensée politique à la fin du Moyen Âge." *Journal des savants*, 1982, no. 2: 169–90.

Kuuliala, Jenni. *Saints, Infirmity, and Community in the Late Middle Ages*. Amsterdam University Press, 2020.

Lantschner, Patrick. *The Logic of Political Conflict in Medieval Cities: Italy and the Southern Low Countries, 1370–1440*. Oxford University Press, 2015.

Laurent, M.-H. "Charles de Blois fut-il canonisé en 1376?" *Revue d'histoire ecclésiastique* 46 (1951): 182–86.

Le Goff, Jacques. "Le mal royal au Moyen Âge: Du roi malade au roi guerisseur." *Mediaevistik* 1 (1988): 101–9.

Lecuppre, Gilles. "Déficience du corps et exercice du pouvoir au XIVe siècle." In "Le corps du prince." Special issue, *Micrologus: Nature, Sciences and Medieval Societies* 22 (2014): 705–19.

Lees, Clare A., ed. *Medieval Masculinities: Regarding Men in the Middle Ages*. University of Minnesota Press, 1994.

Leguay, Jean-Pierre. *Un réseau urbain au Moyen Âge: Les villes du duché de Bretagne aux XIVème et XVème siècles*. Maloine, 1981.

Leguay, Jean-Pierre, and Hervé Martin. *Fastes et malheurs de la Bretagne ducale, 1213–1532*. OuestFrance, 1982.

Lémeillat, Marjolaine. "Jean et Olivier de Bretagne, comtes de Penthièvre, vicomtes de Limoges (1384–1433)." In "La vicomté de Limoges sous les ducs de Bretagne," edited by Yves Coativy and Anne Massoni. Special issue, *Annales de Bretagne et des Pays de l'Ouest* 126, no. 2 (2019): 69–83.

Levasseur, Aurelle. "Dénoncer la tyrannie: Le jeu de l'antagonisme entre l'étranger et le naturel dans le *Pèlerinage de l'Ame* de Guillaume de Digulleville." In *Le Pèlerinage de l'âme de Guillaume de Digulleville (1355–1358): Regards croiseés*, edited by Marie Bassano, Esther Dehoux, and Catherine Vincent, 39–48. Brepols, 2014.

Lewis, Katherine J. "Katherine of Valois: The Vicissitudes of Reputation." In *Later Plantagenet and the Wars of the Roses Consorts: Power, Influence, and Dynasty*, edited by Aidan Norrie, Carolyn Harris, J. L. Laynesmith, Danna R. Messer, and Elena Woodacre, 123–44. Palgrave Macmillan, 2023.

——. *Kingship and Masculinity in Late Medieval England*. Routledge, 2013.

Livingstone, Amy. "Recalculating the Equation: Powerful Woman = Extraordinary." In "Beyond Women and Power: Looking Backward and Moving Forward," edited by Kathy M. Krause. Special issue, *Medieval Feminist Forum* 51, no. 2 (2016): 17–29.

Lobineau, Gui Alexis. *Histoire de Bretagne*. 2 vols. Muguet, 1707.

Lochrie, Karma. *Covert Operations: The Medieval Uses of Secrecy*. University of Pennsylvania Press, 1999.

LoPrete, Kimberly A. "Gendering Viragos: Medieval Perceptions of Powerful Women." In *Gendering the Master Narrative: Women and Power in the Middle Ages*, edited by Mary Erler and Maryanne Kowaleski, 17–38. Cornell University Press, 2003.

——. "Women, Gender and Lordship in France, c.1050–1250." *History Compass* 5 (2007): 1921–1941.

Luce, Siméon. *La France pendant la guerre de Cent Ans*. Hachette, 1890.

Major, J. Russell. "'Bastard Feudalism' and the Kiss: Changing Social Mores in Late Medieval and Early Modern France." *Journal of Interdisciplinary History* 17 (1987): 509–35.

Martin, Carol A. N. "Hoel-Hearted Loyalty and the Ironization of Arthur in Geoffrey's *Historia regum Britanniae*." *Arthuriana* 11 (2001): 21–48.

Martin, Hervé. *Les ordres mendiants en Bretagne (vers 1230–vers 1530): Pauvreté volontaire et prédication à la fin du Moyen-Âge*. Klincksieck, 1975.

Martin, Russell E. "Anticipatory Association of the Heir in Early Modern Russia: Primogeniture and Succession in Russia's Duling Dynasties." In *The Routledge History of Monarchy*, edited by Elena Woodacre, Lucinda H. S. Dean, Chris Jones, Russell E. Martin, and Zita Eva Rohr, 420–42. Routledge, 2019.

Marvin, Julia. "Albine and Isabelle: Regicidal Queens and the Historical Imagination of the Anglo-Norman Prose *Brut* Chronicles." *Arthurian Literature* 18 (2001): 143–91.

Mauger, Michel. *Aristocratie et mécénat en Bretagne au XVe siècle: Jean de Derval, seigneur de Châteaugiron, bâtisseur et bibliophile*. Société archéologique et historique d'Ille-et-Vilaine, 2013.

Mazzei, Valentina. "The Two Claimants and their Champions: War in Brittany in Words and Images in Book I Manuscripts of Froissart's *Chroniques*." In *Battle and Bloodshed: The Medieval World at War*, edited by Keira Borrill and Lorna Bleach, 137–60. Cambridge Scholars, 2013.

McCannon, Afrodesia E. "Two Capetian Queens as the Foreground for an Aristocrat's Anxiety in the *Vie de Saint Louis*." In *Capetian Women*, edited by Kathleen Nolan, 163–76. Palgrave Macmillan, 2003.

McGlynn, Margaret, and Richard J. Moll. "Chaste Marriage in the Middle Ages: 'It Were to Hire a Greet Merite.'" In *Handbook of Medieval Sexuality*, edited by Vern L. Bullough and James A. Brundage, 103–22. 1996. Routledge, 2000.

McNamara, Jo Ann. "The *Herrenfrage*: The Restructuring of the Gender System, 1050–1150." In *Medieval Masculinities: Regarding Men in the Middle Ages*, edited by Clare A. Lees, 3–29. University of Minnesota Press, 1994.

McVitty, E. Amanda. "False Knights and True Men: Contesting Chivalric Masculinity in English Treason Trials, 1388–1415." *Journal of Medieval History* 40 (2014): 458–77.

Metzler, Irina. *Disability in Medieval Europe: Thinking about Physical Impairment during the High Middle Ages, c.1100–1400*. Routledge, 2006.

Morice, Hyacinthe, and Charles Taillandier. *Histoire ecclésiastique et civile de Bretagne*. 2 vols. Delaguette, 1750–1756.

Murray, Jacqueline, ed. *Conflicted Identities and Multiple Masculinities: Men in the Medieval West*. 1999. Routledge, 2011.

Naderer, Max. "Love and Fear: Debating Violence in the Political Culture of the 'Civil War' Period in Norway and Denmark, c. 1130–1240." PhD diss., University of Oslo, 2020.

Nassiet, Michel. "Parenté et successions dynastiques aux XIVe et XVe siècles." *Annales: Économies, sociétés, civilisations* 50 (1995): 621–44.

——. *Parenté, noblesse et États dynastiques, XVe–XVIe siècles*. École des hautes études en sciences sociales, 2000.

Nelson, J. L. "Monks, Secular Men and Masculinity, c. 900." In *Masculinity in Medieval Europe*, edited by D. M. Hadley, 121–42. Routledge, 1999.

Ormrod, W. Mark. "Monarchy, Martyrdom, and Masculinity: England in the Later Middle Ages." In *Holiness and Masculinity in the Middle Ages*, edited by P. H. Cullum and Katherine J. Lewis, 174–91. University of Wales Press, 2004.

——. "The Sexualities of Edward II." In *The Reign of Edward II: New Perspectives*, edited by Gwilym Dodd and Anthony J. Musson, 22–47. York Medieval Press, 2006.

Orning, Hans Jacob. *Constant Crisis: Deconstructing the Civil Wars in Norway, ca. 1180–1220*. Cornell University Press, 2025.

Orning, Hans Jacob, Kim Esmark, and Jón Viðar Sigurðsson, eds. *New Perspectives on the "Civil Wars" in Medieval Scandinavia*. Brepols, 2024.

Orning, Hans Jacob, and Henrik Vigh. "Constant Crisis." In *Medieval and Modern Civil Wars: A Comparative Perspective*, edited by Jón Viðar Sigurðsson and Hans Jacob Orning, 1–33. Brill, 2021.

Palmer, J. J. N. "Book I (1325–78) and Its Sources." In *Froissart: Historian*, edited by J. J. N. Palmer, 7–24. Boydell, 1981.

Parsons, John Carmi. "'Loved Him—Hated Her': Honor and Shame at the Medieval Court." In *Conflicted Identities and Multiple Masculinities: Men in the Medieval West*, edited by Jacqueline Murray, 279–97. 1999. Routledge, 2011.

——. "The Queen's Intercession in Thirteenth-Century England." In *Power of the Weak: Studies on Medieval Women*, edited by Jennifer Carpenter and Sally-Beth MacLean, 147–77. University of Illinois Press, 1995.

Phillips, Joanna. "Crusader Masculinities in Bodily Crises: Incapacity and the Crusader Leader, 1095–1274." In *Crusading and Masculinities*, edited by Natasha R. Hodgson, Katherine J. Lewis, and Matthew M. Mesley, 149–64. Routledge, 2019.

Plaine, François. "De l'autorité de Froissard comme historien des guerres de Bretagne au XIVe siècle, 1341–1364." *Revue de Bretagne et de Vendée* 29 (1871): 5–32, 119–36.

Plassmann, Alheydis. "William of Malmesbury, the *Gesta Stephani*, and the Idea of Successful and Good Rule in the Twelfth Century." In *Anglo-Norman Studies XLV*, edited by S. D. Church, 1–18. Boydell, 2023.

Pocquet du Haut-Jussé, B.-A. *Les papes et les ducs de Bretagne: essai sur les rapports du Saint-Siège avec un État*. 1928. Coop Breizh, 2000.

Rasmussen, Ann Marie, ed. *Rivalrous Masculinities*. University of Notre Dame Press, 2019.

Rohr, Zita Eva, and Lisa Benz, eds. *Queenship, Gender, and Reputation in the Medieval and Early Modern West, 1060–1600*. Palgrave Macmillan, 2016.

Rosenwein, Barbara H. *Emotional Communities in the Early Middle Ages*. Cornell University Press, 2006.

——. "Thinking Historically about Medieval Emotions." *History Compass* 8 (2010): 828–42.

Roux, Brigitte. *Les dialogues de Salmon et Charles VI: Images du pouvoir et enjeux politiques*. Droz, 1998.

Scordia, Lydwine. "*Il n'est pas sire de son pays qui de ses hommes est haï*: Un proverbe sur l'amour et la haine du prince à la fin du Moyen Âge." *Memini* 19–20 (2016): 297–310.

Scott, Joan Wallach. *Gender and the Politics of History*. Revised ed. Columbia University Press, 1999.

Sigurðsson, Jón Viðar, and Hans Jacob Orning. Introduction to *Medieval and Modern Civil Wars: A Comparative Perspective*, ix–xxiii. Brill, 2021.

Sjursen, Katrin E. "Peaceweavers' Sisters: Medieval Noblewomen as Military Leaders in Northern France, 1000–1337." PhD diss., University of California at Santa Barbara, 2010.

——. "Pirate, Traitor, Wife: Jeanne of Belleville and the Categories of Fourteenth-Century French Noblewomen." In *Medieval Elite Women and the Exercise of Power, 1100–1400: Moving Beyond the Exceptionalist Debate*, edited by Heather J. Tanner, 135–56. Palgrave Macmillan, 2019.

———. "The War of the Two Jeannes: Rulership in the Fourteenth Century." *Medieval Feminist Forum* 51, no. 1 (2015): 4–40.

Slater, Laura. "Rumour and Reputation Management in Fourteenth-Century England: Isabella of France in Text and Image." *Journal of Medieval History* 47 (2021): 257–92.

Small, Graeme. *Late Medieval France*. Palgrave Macmillan, 2009.

Smith, Katherine Allen. "Saints in Shining Armor: Martial Asceticism and Masculine Models of Sanctity, ca. 1050–1250." *Speculum* 83 (2008): 572–602.

———. *War and the Making of Medieval Monastic Culture*. Boydell, 2011.

Smoller, Laura Ackerman. "Northern and Southern Sanctity in the Canonization of Vincent Ferrer: The Effects of Procedural Differences on the Image of the Saint." In *Procès de canonisation au Moyen Âge: Aspects juridiques et religieux*, edited by Gábor Klaniczay, 289–308. École française de Rome, 2004.

Snaith, Rhiannon Elizabeth. "The Politics of Noble Reputation in Late Medieval England, 1377–1437." PhD diss., Durham University, 2021.

Soria, Myriam, and Maïté Billoré, eds. *La rumeur au Moyen Âge: Du mépris à la manipulation, Ve–XVe siècle*. Presses universitaires de Rennes, 2011.

Spangler, Jonathan. "A Family Affair: Cultural Anxiety, Political Debate and the Nature of Monarchy in Seventeenth-Century France and Britain." In *The Routledge History of Monarchy*, edited by Elena Woodacre, Lucinda H. S. Dean, Chris Jones, Russell E. Martin, and Zita Eva Rohr, 465–78. Routledge, 2019.

Storey, Gabrielle. "Questioning Terminologies: Homosocial and 'Homosexual' Bonds in the Royal Bedchamber and Kingship in Medieval England and France." *Royal Studies Journal* 9 (2022): 33–45.

Strohm, Paul. *Hochon's Arrow: The Social Imagination of Fourteenth-Century Texts*. Princeton University Press, 1992.

Sullivan, Karen. *The Interrogation of Joan of Arc*. University of Minnesota Press, 1999.

Sumption, Jonathan. *Trial by Battle*. Vol. 1 of *The Hundred Years War*. Faber & Faber, 1999.

Tanner, Heather J. *Medieval Elite Women and the Exercise of Power, 1100–1400: Moving Beyond the Exceptionalist Debate*. Palgrave Macmillan, 2019.

———. "Women's Legal Capacity: Was the Thirteenth Century a Turning Point?" In *Paradigm Shifts in the Middle Ages and Early Modern Age: Transformations, Reformation, and Revolutions in the Pre-Modern World*, edited by Albrecht Classen, 81–98. Brepols, 2019.

Taylor, Andrew. "Chivalric Conversation and the Denial of Male Fear." In *Conflicted Identities and Multiple Masculinities: Men in the Medieval West*, edited by Jacqueline Murray, 169–88. 1999. Routledge, 2011.

Taylor, Craig. *Chivalry and the Ideals of Knighthood in France During the Hundred Years War*. Cambridge University Press, 2013.

———. "The Salic Law, French Queenship, and the Defense of Women in the Late Middle Ages." *French Historical Studies* 29 (2006): 543–64.

———. *A Virtuous Knight: Defending Marshal Boucicaut (Jean II Le Meingre, 1366–1421)*. York Medieval Press, 2019.

Tesnière, Marie-Hélène. "Les manuscrits copiés par Raoul Tainguy: Un aspect de la culture des grands officiers royaux au début du XVe siècle." *Romania* 107 (1986): 282–368.

Théry-Astruc, Julien. "*Fama*: L'opinion publique comme preuve judiciaire. Aperçu sur la révolution médiévale de l'inquisitoire (XIIe–XIVe siècle)." In *La preuve en justice de l'Antiquité à nos jours*, edited by Bruno Lemesle, 119–47. Presses universitaires de Rennes, 2003.

——. "'Fama': Public Opinion as a Legal Category. Inquisitorial Procedure and the Medieval Revolution in Government (12th–14th centuries)." In "'Dicitur': Hearsay in Science, Memory and Poetry." Special issue, *Micrologus* 32 (2024): 153–94.

Thibodeaux, Jennifer D. *The Manly Priest: Clerical Celibacy, Masculinity, and Reform in England and Normandy, 1066–1300*. University of Pennsylvania Press, 2015.

Toynbee, Margaret R. *S. Louis of Toulouse and the Process of Canonisation in the Fourteenth Century*. Manchester University Press, 1929.

Turner, Ralph V. "Eleanor of Aquitaine, Twelfth-Century English Chroniclers and Her 'Black Legend.'" *Nottingham Medieval Studies* 52 (2008): 17–42.

Ueltschi, Karin. *Le pied qui cloche ou le lignage des boiteux*. Champion, 2011.

Vallée-Karcher, Aline. "Jeanne de Bourgogne, épouse de Philippe VI de Valois: Une reine maudite?" *Bibliothèque de l'École des chartes* 138 (1980): 94–96.

Van Engen, John. "Sacred Sanctions for Lordship." In *Cultures of Power: Lordship, Status, and Process in Twelfth-Century Europe*, edited by Thomas N. Bisson, 203–30. University of Pennsylvania Press, 1995.

Vauchez, André. "Canonisation et politique au XIVe siècle: Documents inédits des Archives du Vatican relatifs au procès de canonisation de Charles de Blois, duc de Bretagne († 1364)." In *Miscellanea in onore di Monsignor Martino Giusti*, 2:381–404. Archivio vaticano, 1978.

——. "Dévotion et vie quotidienne à Périgueux au temps de Charles V, d'après un recueil de miracles de Charles de Blois." In *Villes, bonnes villes, cités et capitales: Études d'histoire urbaine (XIIe–XVIIIe siècle) offertes à Bernard Chevalier*, edited by Monique Bourin, 305–14. Paradigme, 1989.

——. "La notion de *miles Christi* dans la spiritualité occidentale aux XIIe et XIIIe siècles." *Chevalerie et christianisme aux XIIe et XIIIe siècles*, edited by Martin Aurell and Catalina Girbea, 67–75. Presses universitaires de Rennes, 2011.

——. *La sainteté en Occident aux derniers siècles du Moyen Âge*. École française de Rome, 1981.

Vermijn, Yvonne. "Chacun son Guesclin: La réception des quatre versions de l'œuvre de Cuvelier entre 1380 et 1480." Master's thesis, University of Utrecht, 2010.

——. "'De quoy juqu'a mille ans bien parlé en sera': La réception de la *Chanson de Bertrand du Guesclin* entre 1380 et 1618." PhD diss., University of Amsterdam, 2018.

Waag, Anaïs. "Rulership, Authority, and Power in the Middle Ages: The Proprietary Queen as Head of Dynasty." In *Anglo-Norman Studies XLIV*, edited by S. D. Church, 71–104. Boydell, 2022.

Walker, Claire, and Heather Kerr, eds. *"Fama" and her Sisters: Gossip and Rumour in Early Modern Europe*. Brepols, 2015.

Watts, John. "Lordship and the State: Alloy or Emulsion?" In *Lordship and the Decentralized State in Late Medieval Europe*, edited by Erika Graham-Goering, Jim van der Meulen, and Frederik Buylaert, 19–39. British Academy, 2025.

——. "The Pressure of the Public on Later Medieval Politics." In *Political Culture in Late Medieval Britain*, edited by Linda Clark and Christine Carpenter, 159–80. Boydell, 2004.

Weissenberg, Marita von. "The Sacrament of Marriage in Late Medieval Hagiography." In *Sacramentum Magnum: Die Ehe in der mittelalterlichen Theologie*, edited by Pavel Blažek, 459–75. Aschendorff, 2018.

Westerhof, Danielle. *Death and the Noble Body in Medieval England*. Boydell, 2008.

Wetzstein, Thomas. "*Iura novit curia*: Zur Verfahrensnormierung der Kanonisationsprozesse des späten Mittelalters." In *Procès de canonisation au Moyen Âge: Aspects juridiques et religieux*, edited by Gábor Klaniczay, 259–88. École française de Rome, 2004.

Whaley, Derek. "From *a* Salic Law to *the* Salic Law: The Creation and Re-creation of the Royal Succession System of France." In *The Routledge History of Monarchy*, edited by Elena Woodacre, Lucinda H. S. Dean, Chris Jones, Russell E. Martin, and Zita Eva Rohr, 443–64. Routledge, 2019.

White, Stephen D. "The Politics of Anger." In *Anger's Past: The Social Uses of an Emotion in the Middle Ages*, edited by Barbara H. Rosenwein, 127–52. Cornell University Press, 1998.

——. *Re-Thinking Kinship and Feudalism in Early Medieval Europe*. Ashgate, 2005.

Wilkinson, Louise J. "Gendered Chivalry." In *A Companion to Chivalry*, edited by Robert W. Jones and Peter R. Coss, 219–39. Boydell, 2019.

Wingard, Tess. "The Trans Middle Ages: Incorporating Transgender and Intersex Studies into the History of Medieval Sexuality." *English Historical Review* 138 (2023): 933–51.

Wittig, Claudia. *Learning to Be Noble in the Middle Ages: Moral Education in North-Western Europe*. Brepols, 2022.

Wolf, Armin. "Reigning Queens in Medieval Europe: When, Where, and Why." In *Medieval Queenship*, edited by John Carmi Parsons, 169–88. 1993. St. Martin's, 1998.

Wood, Charles T. *The French Apanages and the Capetian Monarchy, 1224–1328*. Harvard University Press, 1966.

Woodacre, Elena. "Leonor of Navarre: The Price of Ambition." In *Queenship, Gender, and Reputation in the Medieval and Early Modern West, 1060–1600*, edited by Zita Eva Rohr and Lisa Benz, 161–82. Palgrave Macmillan, 2016.

——. *Queens and Queenship*. Arc Humanities, 2021.

——. *The Queens Regnant of Navarre: Succession, Politics, and Partnership, 1274–1512*. Palgrave Macmillan, 2013.

——. "Understanding the Mechanisms of Monarchy." In *The Routledge History of Monarchy*, edited by Elena Woodacre, Lucinda H. S. Dean, Chris Jones, Russell E. Martin, and Zita Eva Rohr, 1–19. Routledge, 2019.

INDEX